TREVOR HUDDLESTON

A recent photograph of Trevor Huddleston

TREVOR HUDDLESTON

Essays on his Life and Work

Edited by
DEBORAH DUNCAN HONORÉ

Oxford   New York
OXFORD UNIVERSITY PRESS
1988

Oxford University Press, Walton Street, Oxford OX2 6DP
Oxford New York Toronto
Delhi Bombay Calcutta Madras Karachi
Petaling Jaya Singapore Hong Kong Tokyo
Nairobi Dar es Salaam Cape Town
Melbourne Auckland
and associated companies in
Beirut Berlin Ibadan Nicosia

Oxford is a trade mark of Oxford University Press

Published in the United States
by Oxford University Press, New York

British Library Cataloguing in Publication Data
Trevor Huddleston.
1. Church of England. Huddleston, Trevor, 1913–
I. Honoré, Deborah Duncan
283'.092'4
ISBN 0–19–826692–8

Library of Congress Cataloging in Publication Data
Trevor Huddleston: essays on his life and work.
1. Huddleston, Trevor, Bp., 1913–
I. Honoré, Deborah Duncan.
BX5700.6.Z8H847 1988   283'.092'4 [B]   88–1422
ISBN 0–19–826692–8

Set by Hope Services, Abingdon
Printed in Great Britain by
Biddles Ltd., Guildford and King's Lynn

PREFACE

A collection of essays such as this, centred on one person, usually has as its unifying theme the particular gift, intellectual, spiritual, or artistic, through which that person has stimulated the imagination of others. These essays range widely, geographically, in treatment, and in tenor. Their unifying theme may lie in challenge—the challenge posed to established mores by the assertion of the value of each human being and equally the challenge to an individual when social mores deliberately flout this value. This is a process which frequently upsets those who are attached to their privileges and strips the velvet glove from the iron hand.

Whether by chance or choice, or simply because he has never allowed expediency to distort the vision of God's love for each person, Trevor Huddleston has been a stumbling-block to many, to others the head of the corner of a longed-for building. Through his own firm religious belief, he has reawakened a sense of the goal of human life in many who are themselves comfortably placed and have never, perhaps, experienced the humiliation of poverty or racial stigma. He has also gained instant recognition and acceptance from those who have suffered such humiliation. So the contributions to this volume all share, in different ways, concern with the challenge to established positions—political, personal, theological, racial, or social—which the contributors have supported or taken part in. They testify that this sharpened awareness owes much to the influence of Trevor Huddleston.

A brief outline of Huddleston's life may help to orientate readers, many of whom may be familiar with one aspect but not know where and how the rest of his life has been spent. He was born in 1913, and as a young man was greatly influenced by the Christian Socialist movement, whose members worked especially in the London slums, trying to mitigate the endemic

poverty they found there, and to awaken the consciences of the
well-to-do. At Oxford, he read history; afterwards he trained
for the priesthood, then joined the Community of the
Resurrection and in 1941 took monastic vows. In 1943, he was
sent to South Africa to take charge of the Community mission,
centred on the Church of Christ the King in the black
township of Sophiatown, Johannesburg (now the Boxing
Centre in the white suburb of Triomf). In 1949, he was
appointed Provincial of the Order, with headquarters a few
miles away in white Rosettenville. In this position, he was also
responsible for St Peter's School (sometimes called the black
Eton) and for the Theological College. During this time he
also did what he could to make some relaxation and recreation
possible to the blacks in the townships—the Odin Cinema was
opened in Sophiatown and the Huddleston Swimming Baths
built in Orlando, and visiting musicians were persuaded to
give concerts.

However, the accession to power in 1948 of the National
Party, with its avowed intent not only to strengthen the
existing colour bar, but to entrench it by legislation, made
confrontation and protest inevitable. Some of the government
legislation was such that to accept it without protest would
have meant dishonour to the principles at the heart of his
religious life and betrayal of the blacks he served. Two areas of
protest were especially provoking to the government—first his
well-publicized protest at the removal of blacks (who had
freehold rights) from Sophiatown and, second, his decision to
close down the school rather than hand it over to government
control and a syllabus designed to train blacks for inferiority.
The government and its supporters were glad to see him leave
in 1956. His parting shot, however, was the book *Naught for
Your Comfort*, published that year, which has sold all over the
world and deeply influenced perceptions of racial conflict.

After some years at his Community's headquarters at
Mirfield, where he was concerned with the training of novices,
Huddleston was consecrated Bishop of Masasi in Tanganyika
(or Tanzania as it soon became). Here, the difficulty of
transition from British administration to independence and
economic responsibility was greatly increased by the shortage
of Tanzanians with any training. In his vast diocese, rural

poverty and lack of education were two of the most urgent problems. During his years there, a lasting respect and friendship developed between him and Julius Nyerere. He retired in 1968, feeling the time had come for an African bishop to be appointed.

Later on that year, he was appointed Suffragan Bishop of Stepney. Here the poverty was of a very different order: to the existing cultural deprivation and class alienation was being added racism as, following in the footsteps of Huguenot and Jewish immigrants, came Asians and West Indians. Once again he was in a situation of discrimination and prejudice. He turned his energies to fostering the common ground which could break down racial and religious boundaries. This time his protests were aimed at the comfortable English establishment and once again, as in South Africa, those who were oppressed experienced the care and loving personal concern of someone with authority who was on their side. Out of this grew practical foundations of hope such as the Huddleston Centre for the Handicapped.

The next, and last, see to which Huddleston was appointed was that of Mauritius, with the archdiocese of the Indian Ocean added for good measure. This once again proved an enriching experience: for the first time, he was serving a minority religion in an area where Muhammadans and Hindus made up the majority and where Anglicans were outnumbered by Roman Catholics. The atmosphere of peaceful cohabitation gave him the opportunity to learn more of the theology and philosophy of the non-Christian faiths and to see in our isolation from each other a challenge it was vital to face and overcome.

But what has marked Huddleston most deeply and formatively has been his greater encounter in South Africa. So it is not surprising that, although he left over thirty years ago, he has been unremittingly involved with anti-apartheid and its allied causes. He has worked to raise funds, to stimulate awareness and informed support for ways and means to hasten the end of this particularly violent and corrosive abuse of power.

There are some friends and associates of Trevor Huddleston's who have not been able to contribute to this volume, despite their wish to do so. One or two have been prevented by political difficulties in South Africa, others because the pressure on leaders of resistance outside that country in travelling to raise support for and to organize their movements takes a heavy toll of their time and health. This is especially true of Oliver Tambo, president of the exiled ANC. Julius Nyerere gives some idea of these pressures in a letter about his contribution:

(Your letter) when it eventually caught up with me after I returned from visiting seventeen countries in two months . . . drew attention to the fact . . . that the too brief piece I had done in a hurry before our departure had never been revised and sent . . . My difficulty was that the request could not have come at a worse moment, so my contribution is not what I would have liked to have written had I had more time. In particular, it does not discuss the situation in Southern Africa . . .

Many (most) of those who have contributed are extremely busy, and the fact that they have made time to produce their essays is a tribute not just to the cause that Trevor Huddleston has made his, but to the mark he has made on their lives.

Oxford University Press is grateful to Bailey's African Photo Archives for permission to reproduce photographs of Huddleston during his time in South Africa. I would like to express my gratitude to the Press for suggesting that I undertake to edit the book, and for providing Anne Ashby as a guide and help.

D.D.H.

CONTENTS

LIST OF CONTRIBUTORS

BOWKER, JOHN WESTERDALE. Adjunct Professor in the universities of North Carolina and Pennsylvania since 1986, and Fellow and Dean of Chapel of Trinity College, Cambridge since 1984; Professor of Religious Studies in the University of Lancaster 1974–85. His essay is based on a paper he contributed to a conference attended by representatives of the major religious faiths, which led to the United Nations Declaration on Religions and Apartheid. He has written *Targums and Jewish Literature* (1969), *Problems of Suffering in the Religions of the World* (1970), *The Sense of God* (1973), and (ed.) *Violence and Aggression* (1983).

CARTER, JAMES ROGER. Graduated from Cambridge and went on to adult education work in London and South Wales 1933–44, though he spent 1938–9 in Berlin as representative of the Society of Friends, concerned with help for persecuted non-Aryans. From 1944 to 1947 he worked with UNRRA in the London division, rehabilitating displaced persons. From 1947 to 1960 he was in the Ministry of Education, and in 1960 was appointed Principal of the Kaimosi Training College, Kenya. Here he was also concerned with preparing the recommendations for education which were incorporated in the new legislation. From 1967 to 1974 he was Ford Foundation adviser on educational planning in Tanzania. He founded the Britain–Tanzania Society in 1974 and is now Vice-Chairman of the United Kingdom chapter.

DENNISTON, ROBIN ALASTAIR. Since 1984 the Oxford Publisher and Senior Deputy Secretary to the Delegates of Oxford University Press. After national service in 1948, he joined Collins as an editor and worked there 1950–9; during this time he was instrumental in publishing *Naught for Your Comfort*. From then on, he held posts of increasing responsibility with several publishing houses until in 1975 he was made Director of Thomson Publications, and Chairman of Michael Joseph, Thomas Nelson, and others. He joined Oxford University Press as Academic Publisher in 1978. Also in 1978, he was ordained deacon, and priest in 1979.

GORDIMER, NADINE. A South African author living in Johannesburg. Since the appearance of her first short stories *The Soft Voice of the Serpent* and her novel *The Lying Days*, both in 1953, she has been accorded an international reputation and has been the recipient of numerous honours in Britain, Europe, and the United States.

LEECH, KENNETH. Director of the Runnymede Trust, a research and information unit on race and immigration issues, based in London. He was Rector of St Matthew's, Bethnal Green, 1974–80, and Race Relations Field Officer of the Church of England's Board for Social Responsibility 1981–7. He is the author of numerous books including *Pastoral Care and the Drug Scene* (1970), *Youthquake* (1973), *Brick Lane 1978* (1980), and *Spirituality and Pastoral Care* (1986).

MacKINNON, DONALD MacKENZIE. A contemporary of Huddleston's at Oxford. He taught philosophy in the universities of Edinburgh and Oxford; from 1947 to 1960 he was Regius Professor of Moral Philosophy at Aberdeen and then from 1960 to 1978 Norris-Hulse Professor of Divinity at Cambridge. He is the author of such books as *The Notion of Philosophy in History* (1954), *The Stripping of Altars* (1969), and *Problems of Metaphysics* (1974). His public lectures include the Scott Holland (1952), the Hobhouse (1953), and the Gifford (1965–6).

MINTY, ABDUL SAMAD. A South African who came to Britain in 1958 and, together with others, founded the Anti-apartheid Movement (AAM) of which he has been the honorary secretary for over 20 years. He has been active in international anti-apartheid campaigns, participated in numerous UN and other conferences, lobbied governments and organizations and addressed UN bodies including the Security Council. Since 1979 he has also been Director of the World Campaign Against Military and Nuclear Collaboration with South Africa, which was initiated by the AAM at the suggestion of the UN Special Committee Against Apartheid.

Nyerere, Julius Kambarage. Leader of the Tanganyika African National Union (TANU) from 1954. From independence in 1962, he became first President of Tanganyika, now Tanzania (as it became upon union with Zanzibar in 1964), until he retired in 1985. Until 1954, after graduating from Makerere University College and Edinburgh University, he was a teacher. He has written *Freedom and Unity* (1966), *Freedom and Socialism* (1969), *Essays on Socialism* (1969), *Freedom and Development* (1973), and has translated Shakespeare's *Julius Caesar* and *The Merchant of Venice* into Swahili. In 1984, he was appointed Chairman of the Organization of African Unity and is now Chairman of the South Commission.

Piachaud, François. Prebendary of St Paul's, is a parish priest who was Vicar of Christ Church, Chelsea, for many years before he retired in 1986. Earlier, he had worked in Leeds, Edinburgh (St John's), and Newcastle upon Tyne. While in Chelsea he was for seven years Director of Clerical and Post-ordination Studies for the London diocese, and later, for fifteen years, a member of the General Synod. His parish work—and he regards the parish as the front line of the Church—has been his principal preoccupation.

Ramphal, Shridath Surendranath. Has since 1975 been Secretary-General of the Commonwealth. After taking a law degree at King's College, London, he returned to Guyana (then British Guiana) and held increasingly responsible legal positions in the administration of his own country, as it worked towards independence, and of the emerging federation of the West Indies. He became Guyana's Minister of State for External Affairs in 1967, and for Foreign Affairs and Justice in 1973. He was knighted in 1970, before Guyana achieved independence. He is much in demand as a public lecturer and on international committees, especially those concerned with development and world poverty. Since 1977 he has been Vice-Chairman of the Centre for Research on the New International Economic Order. His book *One World to Share* (1979) reflects this concern. In 1986, he was a member of the Commonwealth Eminent Persons Group which visited South Africa.

Ranger, Terence. Educated at Oxford, he went on to teach at the Royal Naval College in Dartmouth. In 1957 he was appointed to the University College of Rhodesia and Nyasaland to teach history. During this time, he edited a journal *Dissent*, which showed the extent to which racial discrimination still existed. In 1963, he was declared a prohibited immigrant, and accepted an appointment to the first Chair of History in the University of East Africa at Dar es Salaam. In 1969, he became Professor of African History in the University of California, Los Angeles, and in 1974 returned to England as the first Africanist to hold the chair of Modern History at Manchester. In 1987, he was appointed Rhodes Professor of Race Relations in Oxford.

THOMPSON, JAMES LAWTON. Ordained in 1966 after leaving the army in 1961. He was appointed Chaplain of Cuddesdon Theological College in 1968, and Rector of Thamesmead in 1971. In 1978, he succeeded Huddleston as Suffragan Bishop of Stepney.

TUTU, DESMOND MPILO. Did his theological training at St Peter's Theological College and was ordained priest in 1961, serving parishes in both South Africa and England. He lectured at the Theological Seminary at Alice, Cape Province, and later at the University of Roma in Lesotho. In 1975, he was appointed Dean of Johannesburg, and in 1976 consecrated Bishop of Lesotho. In 1978, he became Assistant Bishop of Johannesburg and also Rector of St Augustine's in Soweto until 1985, when he was made Bishop of Johannesburg. In 1986, he was consecrated Archbishop of Cape Town, and thus became the first black to be head of the Anglican Church in South Africa. He has written *Crying in the Wilderness* (1982) and *Hope and Suffering* (1983).

WEBB, PAULINE MARY. Has recently retired from the post of Organiser of Religious Broadcasting, BBC World Service. Educated at King's College, London, she started her career in teaching, then went on to hold increasingly responsible administrative posts in the Methodist Church, especially in the field of missionary work and lay activity. She was appointed Vice-Chairman of the Central Committee of the World Council of Churches in 1968, and in 1976 Chairman of the BBC Community and Race Relations Unit. She has written many books concerned with religion in contemporary society of which the most recent is *Faith and Faithfulness* (1985).

WILLIAMS, ROWAN DOUGLAS. Has been the Lady Margaret Professor of Divinity in the University of Oxford and a Canon of Christ Church since 1986. He took a degree at Cambridge and a D.Phil. at Oxford and subsequently became a lecturer in divinity in Cambridge in 1980, and a Fellow and Dean of Clare College 1984–6. His books include *The Wound of Knowledge* (1979), *Resurrection* (1982), and *Truce of God* (1983).

LIST OF ILLUSTRATIONS

Frontispiece A recent photograph of Trevor Huddleston, taken at a conference. By permission of the USPG.

An Appreciation of the Rt. Revd Trevor Huddleston, CR

DESMOND TUTU

WHEN did I first meet Father Trevor Huddleston? Oh, he was father to so many in Sophiatown. I thought it was when I started school in 1944 in what was called Western Native Township; it is now Western Coloured Township in our country obsessed with colour and race. It was a high school started by Father Raymond Raynes when he was priest-in-charge of Christ the King in Sophiatown, a position in which Father Trevor succeeded him. This would have been in 1945, at the end of World War II. Father Huddleston came to our school to speak on VE day and I was always amused at how he pronounced 'Nazi'. I thought he didn't know how to pronounce. But actually that was not the first time I met him.

The very first time was when I was a boy of about 8 or 9. My mother was working as a domestic worker/cook in the hostel for black blind women at the Blind Institute called Ezenzeleni, 'place where you do things for yourself', meant to encourage black blind people not to feel sorry for themselves but to know that they could achieve. This institute had been started by a remarkable English couple, Arthur and Florence Blaxall. We were standing with my mother on the balcony of the women's hostel where she was cook when this white man in a big black hat and a white flowing cassock swept past on the way to the residence of the Blaxalls. You could have knocked me down with a feather, young as I was at the time, when this man doffed his hat to my mother; I couldn't understand a white man doffing his hat to a black woman, an

uneducated woman. At the time, of course, it was just an
incident among many which one thought one had forgotten;
but it made, it appeared later, a very deep impression on me
and said a very great deal about the person who had done this.
For it was, as I later discovered, none other than Father
Huddleston, who had come to be priest-in-charge of Christ
the King Church and prior of Christ the King Priory of the
Community of the Resurrection.

I came to live in a hostel which the Fathers opened for
young men who were working or at high school and had
problems with accommodation. It saved my parents a fair
amount of money, in that I did not have to be travelling every
day between Krugersdorp and school, a distance of about
thirty miles each way by train. And so I got to know Father
Trevor a little better. In fact I made my first real sacramental
confession to him, and perhaps that began a very close
relationship between him and me. It was not exclusive,
because he had so many other people who looked to him,
many other people he cared for. He was so un-English in
many ways, being very fond of hugging people, embracing
them, and in the way in which he laughed. He did not laugh
like many white people, only with their teeth, he laughed with
his whole body, his whole being, and that endeared him very
much to black people. And if he wore a white cassock it did
not remain clean for long, as he trudged the dusty streets of
Sophiatown with the little urchins with grubby fingers always
wanting to touch him and calling out 'Fader' with obvious
affection in their little voices. He loved us—tremendous. He
was fond of letting you sit on his lap, and in 1978 when I told
people at the Lambeth Conference that I used to sit on
Trevor's lap, they looked at me looking so decrepit and him
still very sprightly, and I don't think they believed me. He
touched many people.

His office in Sophiatown would have very many street
urchins playing marbles on the floor and the next moment when
he had shooed them out he would be meeting ambassadors
and high-placed officials and leading businessmen. He had a
very close relationship with Alan Paton, who at the time was
running the Diepkloof Reformatory, near where we now have
a huge hospital, Baragwanath Hospital, just south of Soweto.

The white priest in *Cry, the Beloved Country* is probably modelled on Trevor Huddleston.

I know that he is a man of very deep prayer and that is what sustained him in his campaigns to alleviate the sorry lot of the people that he loved so very dearly. He was a spellbinding speaker as he sought to raise the consciousness of South African whites to the plight of blacks, and he was very much in the forefront in the struggle to save Sophiatown when in 1948 the Nationalist government came to power. Dr Verwoerd was then in charge of what was called Native Affairs and set as his object the destruction of Sophiatown, because it was an anomaly in their policy which regarded all black people as birds of passage, temporary denizens of the white man's town. Sophiatown stuck out as a sore thumb because, there, blacks had what was unacceptable, freehold title to their land.

Father Huddleston helped to galvanize the people in their efforts to resist this, the first move to destroy a stable black community, the first of many such instances. To date this government has uprooted over three million people. You know that Sophiatown was killed and the white suburb which replaced Sophiatown was called in Afrikaans ' Triomf'. With the subtlety of a bull in a china shop, to rub salt into the wounds of black people who had seen their life's savings going down the drain with the destruction of the homes they had built so painstakingly, many of the street names in Triomf are the street names of the old Sophiatown streets. So many of us who lived in that teeming, bustling place, when we drive through Triomf, drive through Ray Street, Annandale, Meyer Street. I shall never forget what this government did to our people. And Trevor sought to stop that great indignity to people he loved very deeply. He was among those who participated in one of the great political highlights of this country in this century, the signing in 1955 of the Freedom Charter, which set out the ideals for a non-racial democratic South Africa; and Trevor was held in such high regard that he was given the highest award that our people could give: a matted ring worn by great warriors at the back of their heads, a kind of halo.

We just want to thank God so very much for the wonderful, wonderful person who made us blacks realize that not all whites were the same. There are many whites who care about justice, about peace, about people, who care about people very much. I was in hospital for twenty months with TB, and if Father Huddleston was in Johannesburg he made it a point to visit me at least once a week during those twenty months. I was just a nonentity, 13 years old, and yet he paid so much attention to me. He touched my life and I am certain that I owe a very, very great deal to him as I do to so many others. He has touched the lives of many others: the present Archbishop of Central Africa was one of his creatures, as he used to call us. Hugh Masekela, the jazz trumpeter, got his first trumpet from Father Huddleston, who had got it as a gift from Louis Satchmo Armstrong, as only he could. But there are many, many others that one could name who were probably set on the road to their ultimate vocation by this remarkable man.

And if blacks still talk to white people, an extraordinary miracle in present-day South Africa, then it will be in large measure due to people like Trevor who made us realize that we too count, we too matter in the sight of God, we too even when we are black are people to whom hats ought to be doffed.

Huddleston: A Sign

NADINE GORDIMER

ABOVE this desk at which I write there are children's paint-
ings, a poster showing Marcel Proust as a small boy with a
large bow-tie and a watch-chain, a carving from the Central
African Republic that looks like a human sundial, and a
photograph. These are my treasures, under whose signs I
spend my working life.

The photograph was taken by my friend David Goldblatt at
the beginning of his career, in 1952, at the Newclare squatter
camp, Johannesburg. It is a night scene, lit only by a tin
brazier. The light from lozenges of incandescent coal brings
forward out of the dark a pair of gaunt, tightly clasped hands,
the long fingers tautly interlaced, making a great double fist.
They are the hands of a white man. Above them there is
darkness again, until the furthermost reach of light leaps on
the bright white band of a clerical collar, and, more softly,
brings from oblivion the three-quarter face. There is a pointed
ear standing alertly away from the head and lean jaw, and the
tendon from behind the ear down the neck is prominent and
tense. The ear is cocked intently and the eyes are concentrated.

The man is the young Father Trevor Huddleston. He is
listening to and looking at someone you can't make out—a
faint lick of light touching knuckles and thumb held towards
the fire, a shirt collar framing the knot of a tie, and above that
a shape almost one with the night, unrecognizable as a face.
But the man, the black man, is there; he is there in the
extraordinary, still, self-excluding attention of the young

priest. Trevor Huddleston's immense *awareness* of black
people, in a city and country and time when white people
ignored their lives, categorized them as so many statistics,
planned to move them about as so many plastic pins on a
demographic map, is in the photograph. It is there as an
emblem of the Defiance Campaign, in which Huddleston had
currently engaged that attention of his, and which the whites
in power crushed while their supporters turned their heads
away. It is there as an omen of what was to come: Sharpeville,
at the start of a new decade; the 1976 uprising; the school,
rent, and shop boycotts, the troops in the black townships, the
detention of thousands without respect for childhood or old
age, the strikes in factories and mines—and the deaths, the
deaths, the unrolling death-scroll of constantly intensified
state violence that, in the 1980s, inevitably brought forth
counter-violence from its victims. Within the chiaroscuro of
that photograph the black people of South Africa are wholly
present in the attention of a white man who, from the
beginning of his experience in our country, saw them not as
statistics and movable counters in some ugly and insane plan
to keep races apart and class domination in power, but as
blood, heart, brain, and spirit, as human beings dispossessed
of their birthright and certain to regain it.

   That is what is in the instant of a night in Newclare in 1952.
I have no religious faith, but when I look at that photograph
of a profoundly religious man, I see godliness in a way I can
understand deeply, I see a man in whom prayer functions, in
Simone Weil's definition,[1] as a special form of intelligent
concentration. Everything that is in that photograph is what
whites in South Africa have turned away from, towards
deliberate fragmentation, callous and stupid denial, wild
political distraction, mindless elevation of indifference; turned
away to catastrophe.

   Yet Trevor Huddleston's concentration remains. It asserts,

---

[1] '. . . prayer consists of attention . . . Not only does the love of God have
attention for its substance; the love of our neighbour, which we know to be
the same love, is made of this same substance. . . . The capacity to give one's
attention to a sufferer is a very rare and difficult thing; it is almost a miracle;
it is a miracle. . . . Warmth of heart . . . pity, are not enough.' Simone Weil,
Waiting on God (London, 1951), 51, 58.

always, that another way of thinking and living existed, and still exists. What is asserted there was passed on by Huddleston to many people and has never been forgotten or abandoned by them, but handed down to another generation. He belongs to the living history of the liberation movement in an ancestry all of us, black and white, who are involved in the movement now are inspired to claim. He is the only white man to have received the *Isitwalandwe*—the highest distinction in African society; that award was conferred upon him in a particular context at the Congress of the People in 1955, but I know of no one in any of the liberation organizations who, whatever their political ideology, does not revere him. Certainly, all whites in the struggle are under his sign.

Everyone in the contemporary world is familiar with the old pious condemnation of churchmen who 'meddle in politics'. In South Africa, it was invoked against the Reverend Michael Scott before Huddleston, and after Huddleston against Bishop Ambrose Reeves and others, as it is now against the Reverend Allan Boesak and (and how!) Archbishop Desmond Tutu. There is a more subtle and sophisticated form of attack— derogation. Its vocabulary, too, is worn smooth: 'sentimental liberalism', 'starry-eyed Utopianism'. 'Priests and pinkos' don't understand that politics is the 'art of the possible'. The inference is always that churchmen who accept political action as part of their responsibility for humankind are well meaning but unfitted for the task. In short, they lack the necessary specific intelligence.

Trevor Huddleston's place in South African history demonstrates exactly the reverse. In him, early on, it was clear that 'intelligence' in all its senses has combined to produce exactly what would have been *the* specific intelligence necessary to find a peaceful political end to racism in all its avatars, economic, social, religious. Intelligence means superior under-standing and quickness of apprehension; inherent mental qualities. It also means what may be acquired: to have intelligence of something is to have news and knowledge of it. Then there is the dimension of Simone Weil's definition: the faculty of 'intelligent concentration' that is prayer. Trevor Huddleston summoned all three into synthesis. (How evident this is in his book, *Naught for your Comfort*.) His actions showed

a superior understanding of the political future of South Africa
far in advance not only of Parliament but also of most liberal
thinkers among people who had the vote—the white minority.
Those actions were based on the first-hand knowledge,
'intelligence', gained working among the majority—the black
South Africans whose lives were to be the decisive factor in
South African politics. Through the focus of his Weilian
faculty, he saw us all clearly, as few of us saw ourselves.

Some of the non-violent forms of resistance that have been
seen to bring results, since, stem from his kind of specific
intelligence. He saw before anyone else that a sports boycott
would rudely waken the average 'non-political' white voter
from the sleep of complacent tacit racism. His initiative has
resulted in the most successful and long-lived anti-apartheid
campaign ever sustained. His political action, supporting the
ANC, encouraging the people of his parish in Sophiatown to
resist one of the first population removals, was evidence of a
prescient understanding and political forecast of what was to
come: the vast and terrible shifting of whole populations, let
alone townships, about the country, the isolation of people in
ethnic backwaters dubbed 'states', the destruction of community
life, and, finally, the stripping of black South Africans of their
citizenship.

He was a good politician, that churchman. If our professional
politicians had had his intelligence they would not have
behind them today the failed Verwoerdian 'grand apartheid';
with them, the doomed Outhouses of Parliament for so-called
Coloureds and Indians only; and ahead an immediate future
that, because of 'reforms' whose scenario is still projected in
black and white, and whose script still keeps ultimate power
in white hands only, promises only violence. Their tragic lack
of intelligence—not being able to grasp the fact of the social
forces of their own post-colonial era, not being open to the
information that the majority was plainly giving them, not
having any political morality other than that based on physical
attributes of skin and hair—has brought this tragedy about.

I didn't know Trevor Huddleston well, personally. I met
him in the early 1950s through our mutual friend Anthony
Sampson, and, set beside my great admiration for the public
figure, there is an endearing trivial memory. Some years later

a party for Anthony Sampson was held in my house. While my husband Reinhold Cassirer and I were still preparing food and drink, the first guest arrived. It was Huddleston, and he and Anthony settled on the verandah. Our son, taking on hostly duties for the first time, kept offering a plate of stuffed eggs, and to his dismay the guest never refused, but kept absently reaching out and eating them. The small boy came rushing indignantly into the kitchen: 'Mum, the man in a skirt is finishing all the eggs!'

An uncharacteristic side-glance at that figure striding so ascetically through our lives in Johannesburg in the 1950s, less at home in white suburbia than in the Sophiatown of crowded yards, shebeens, vigorous street life, the blare of *pata-pata* music, and the roof-raising voices of the congregation singing in the people's lovely home on the hill, his Church of Christ the King. But wherever I encountered him, here or there, 'the man in a skirt' was an assurance that South Africa didn't have to be as it was, that the barriers set up between black and white must come down in situations other and greater than private affinities and friendships—those relationships which many of us in the 1950s enjoyed but which lacked the necessary political energy and dedication to bring freedom.

He left us, left South Africa physically. It was not of his own volition. But he hasn't gone, any more than Mandela, Sisulu, Mbeki, Kathrada, and their fellow prisoners are not with us. He acted here, and has continued to act in exile, to achieve a different South Africa, which he knew was and knows is possible, and will be.

Challenges in a
Poor Country

JULIUS K. NYERERE

WHEN Trevor Huddleston was chosen as the Bishop of
Masasi in Southern Tanzania in 1960, very many non-
Anglicans in the Nationalist Movement—Muslims as well as
Christians—were pleased. We regarded this appointment as a
progressive one, indicating a desire on the part of the Anglican
authorities to co-operate with the people of Tanganyika on
terms of human equality. It seemed to be a good augury for
our approaching independence.

In adopting that attitude we were not meaning to criticize
either the earlier bishops of Masasi or other missionaries. My
country has, on the whole, been well served by religious
leaders and workers of many different denominations; a
considerable number of missionaries won great affection as
well as respect for themselves from the people in their area of
service.

Yet I think it is not unfair to say that until then the
prevailing missionary approach had been one of paternalism,
of serving God by doing things *for* the Africans, but as a
general rule not identifying with them and using greater
knowledge to help them do for themselves the things they
wanted to do. It has to be remembered that, although the
Trusteeship Territory of Tanganyika never suffered under
anything like apartheid, there were areas where Africans
lived, and others where Europeans lived; there were European
schools and hospitals, Asian schools and hospitals, and African

schools and hospitals, and there was very little social or work mixing on the basis of equality.

Separate racial structures were very quickly brought to an end after independence in 1961. But attitudes do not so quickly change—and the abysmally low level of education, and the extreme poverty, could not be overcome simply by new legislation or administrative fiat. The knowledge that Trevor Huddleston was coming to work in our country suggested to us in the Nationalist Movement that we were getting a Church leader who would be a new and understanding ally in the pursuit of our ambitions to secure and consolidate our independence, and to build a non-racial society based on the people's development by their own efforts.

For political consciousness was very widespread in Tanganyika by 1960, and we already knew Trevor Huddleston by reputation. In particular we knew of his work in South Africa—from Africans of South Africa, as well as from political friends in the United Kingdom. And some of us had read his book *Naught for Your Comfort*; we knew that he had continued to campaign for the rights of the people of South Africa even after leaving that country. He was an active worker in the struggle against racism; so he was our friend, because he was a friend of our cause, before he ever set foot in Tanzania.

The poverty which Bishop Huddleston met in Masasi was very different in nature from that with which he was familiar in Johannesburg. In Masasi it was rural poverty—people living from season to season with their subsistence depending upon whether the rains were good and what they could produce on their own plots. And Masasi was an area with virtually no public utility services apart from the electricity and water supplies which the mission stations had established for their own needs. Such medical services and schools as existed in the area were also very largely those provided by the different missions, and the people tended to live in scattered homesteads. The poverty of Masasi—as indeed of Tanzania as a whole—was the poverty of underdevelopment. Even surface communications between Masasi and the capital city were (and still are) virtually non-existent for many months of the year. Despite many advances, Tanzania still suffers from the poverty of underdevelopment.

The details of Bishop Huddleston's work within his diocese are known to those who worked in the Church with him, and who took over from him when he left. For he worked hard to develop the knowledge, the experience, and the self-confidence of Church ministers, and of lay persons in his Church; as a result of his efforts he could be replaced by a Tanzanian bishop. At the same time Bishop Huddleston co-operated positively with the young and inexperienced political and administrative leaders in the region after independence, as well as building good relations with central government.

I met the new bishop when he first arrived in Tanganyika; the fact that he sought me out was itself indicative of his attitude towards our future. For I was the leader of the Nationalist Movement, and independence was still more than a year ahead; the colonial government had not by then accepted our demand for independence in 1961, and a smooth transition was therefore still not assured.

But of those early years before and after independence, four things stand out in my memory in relation to Bishop Huddleston's relations with our young government. The first is his co-operative response when government decided to take over from the missions all responsibility for, and running of, primary and secondary mission schools.

He had quickly realized that, even after the missions had opened their schools to non-Christians, devout Muslims were not prepared to send their children to Christian-run schools, and also that all non-Christians were at a disadvantage when so large a proportion of 'African education' was in mission hands. The bishop therefore understood that the government had a positive purpose in its decision, and was not taking an 'anti-religious' position. That purpose was to strengthen national unity by means of a common curriculum throughout the country, and at the same time to take another step inhibiting the growth of political divisions between Christians on the one hand and Muslims and other non-Christians on the other.

The second action by the bishop which stands out as I look

back is the manner in which he initiated and worked for the establishment of an agricultural training centre for the young people of Masasi. He could have done this—as many other missionaries did before and after that time—as a purely mission activity. It would have been as useful to the young men and women who went there! Such a method might also have been easier, and resulted in a quicker outcome more absolutely in line with his own vision of what was needed. But Bishop Huddleston involved the Party and the Government officials in the activity, as well as people of his own Church; as a result all of them felt proud of its establishment, and it was Party leaders who insisted that I visit it during one of my tours in the district. Bishop Huddleston faced up to the challenge of working with Tanzanians, and through the somewhat cumbersome and inefficient machinery of our young state.

A third memory is of Bishop Huddleston in public disagreement with the government. It was a few years after independence, and both government and people had become very concerned about growing theft of public property, especially by people in positions of responsibility. Our reaction was a common one—to increase the penalties on conviction. And in our case the penalty introduced in new legislation was a minimum jail sentence plus twelve strokes at the beginning of the sentence and twelve immediately before release. The bishop used the opportunity of a sermon in Dar es Salaam (although he rarely preached in the capital) to oppose the proposed penalties, and his sermon was reported in the newspapers; I suspect he had invited the reporters!

Ours is a democratic one-party State, but still a young one, and there were a number of political leaders who were extremely critical of what they regarded as interference in the political process by an expatriate bishop! Others, however, said in effect: well, it is Bishop Huddleston and he always says what he believes to be right, but he's on our side in the struggle for justice and human dignity in Africa. The Bill was passed, and implemented; but what he said about corporal punishment being inconsistent with human dignity made its mark and was not forgotten. After a few years government itself introduced an amendment to the Act so as to delete the corporal punishment element of the penalty—which the prison service had always heartily disliked. On the second attempt (the first having been defeated by the Legislature) the amendment was passed by Parliament.

My fourth outstanding memory does not relate directly to Bishop Huddleston's relations with the Tanzanian government, but rather to his relations with the British one. Given his background in South Africa, it was inevitable that he should follow very closely the buildup to UDI by the Smith regime in Rhodesia, and its announcement in November 1965. The British inaction in response to these events made him very upset. He felt that his own country—the nation of which he was a citizen—was compromising on the question of racism and he wanted to make a strong personal protest. It was Tanzanians who persuaded him that as a bishop in Tanzania he should leave public action to the Tanzanian government; none the less, his genuine anger was both understood and appreciated.

Bishop Huddleston left Tanzania in 1968. As he had hoped, he was replaced by a Tanzanian bishop. But neither he nor, I think, the lessons he taught have been forgotten by the people of that diocese or by other Tanzanians who had the good fortune to come into contact with him. In less than eight years he became one of 'our people'; his rare visits to Masasi since then have been occasions of very great pleasure to the people there.

But this has not been the sum total of Bishop Huddleston's continuing contact with Tanzania. As the President of the Britain–Tanzania Society he has been able to continue to work with others—both other British friends of our country and Tanzanians—to help a number of villages acquire the kind of simple tools or equipment with which the people can develop themselves and their environment more quickly than they could do unaided. And he and his colleagues in the British chapter of that Society have on many occasions used their knowledge of Tanzania and Tanzanians to try to promote understanding of the purposes of our policies—both economic and international.

But never at any time has Bishop Huddleston forgotten the people among whom he worked in South Africa. Throughout his active work for the people of Masasi, Bishop Huddleston remained in contact with the anti-apartheid struggle—not a very difficult thing to do from Dar es Salaam, where all the nationalist movements in Southern Africa had offices, but certainly not easy from Masasi in Southern Tanzania, owing to our poor communications. And since he returned to Britain, his active presidency of the Anti-apartheid Movement has been one of the many points of contact between him and Tanzania.

For I think both we in Tanzania and the bishop himself regarded his work in our country and his work in South Africa as two aspects of a single task. That task was to respond to the challenge of human development so that men and women can live in conditions of dignity, self-respect, and justice. Apartheid is in fundamental opposition to all these principles; so is the poverty of underdevelopment, leading to ignorance and disease.

Bishop Huddleston has been, and still is, a fighter in the struggle for the triumph of human equality and dignity in Africa. He is also a human being who exudes warmth and friendship towards the men, women, and children whom he meets; he enriches the lives of those with whom he works.

He meets the challenges of life with confidence and faith: he is an encouragement to us all.

Anglo-Tanzanian Relations

J. ROGER CARTER

ANGLO-TANZANIAN relations deserve our attention not only because their course since independence has coincided with the presidency of one of Africa's outstanding leaders, but also because they display features common to the post-imperial relations of many of Britain's former colonies with the erstwhile mother country. Tanzania's relations with, for example, the countries of Scandinavia have never been encumbered by a colonial taint and have remained straight-forward and friendly. But the relationship with the former masters has always been much more complex, more akin to the relations between strong-minded members of the same family. As one Tanzanian once confessed, he preferred the devil he knew to the devil he didn't know. But this aphorism hardly does justice either to the complexity, or to the scope, of the relationship. Tanzanians knew their way round with the British, understood their language. Some had received their higher education in Britain. The institutions of state that they took over at independence were fashioned according to British usage and some, notably the institutions of justice, have survived largely unchanged to this day. In general, the Tanzanian reaction to their former masters was forgiving and generous, but there were times when the British government's behaviour was beyond their comprehension. While the restrictions on Britain's room for manœuvre created by her historic economic relations with South Africa did not pass unacknowledged, the suggestion, as Tanzanians saw it, that

Britain was making profits at the expense of the oppressed
African majority and was undermining the struggle against
apartheid was too painful to conceal.

The communiqué issued at the close of the Constitutional
Conference leading to the independence of Tanganyika in
December 1961 included the following words: 'The Conference
declared their faith that the close and friendly ties between the
two countries, which were ensuring smooth and rapid progress
to independence, would be continued in the future between an
independent Tanganyika and the United Kingdom.'[1] A
month earlier, Mr Iain Macleod, the Secretary of State for the
Colonies, said in the House of Commons that 'Tanganyika is
one of the most splendid and exciting examples of progress in
Africa. It has been so for many years and will, I hope,
continue.'[2] During the debate on the aid programme two
months after the introduction of self-government, Mr Marquand
asked the Secretary of State 'to bear in mind that Tanganyika
is the poorest of the three East African territories, that it is
giving a shining example of non-racialism and that it deserves
well from this country', to which Mr Macleod replied, 'I am
certain that everyone in this House echoes that. We have had
it very much in mind in our discussions.'[3]

But this euphoric atmosphere was not to last. On 15
December 1965, almost exactly four years after independence,
Tanzania (as Tanganyika had then become) broke off
diplomatic relations with the United Kingdom. When they
were resumed in 1968 a more hard-headed attitude towards
formal relationships had supervened. Nevertheless, imperfect
mutual understanding continued to deny the hopes entertained
at independence and to provide grounds for irritation and
mistrust.

At the time of independence it was not clearly foreseen that
relations with a former colonial power were bound to be
fragile and that adjustments would be needed on both sides if
earlier expectations were to be fulfilled. In the first years of
independence Tanganyika remained heavily dependent on

[1] Hansard 638, cols. 14–15, 11 Apr. 1961.
[2] Iain Macleod, Colonial Secretary, Hansard 636, col. 674, 9 Mar. 1961.
[3] David Marquand and Iain Macleod, Hansard 644, col. 578, 13 July
1961.

British personnel for almost all senior posts in the administration. At the time of internal self-government on 15 May 1961 all Permanent Secretaries, all Provincial Commissioners, 55 out of 57 District Commissioners, all class II officers in government service, and 248 out of 264 class III officers were British. Out of 75 senior and middle-ranking officers in the Treasury in September 1961 only two were Africans.[4] At independence only 17 per cent of middle- and higher-level posts in government were occupied by Tanzanians and out of 630 graduate teachers in secondary schools only 20 were African graduates.[5] In the period between independence and 30 June 1966 some 674 expatriates were recruited for government service, of whom 549 were from the United Kingdom.[6]

Such dependence on the citizens of the former colonial power naturally aroused misgivings in many quarters and was seen as a serious inroad into Tanzania's newly won sovereign independence. However, initially the retention in service of a large number of expatriates was inevitable and Julius Nyerere, the Prime Minister, did what he could to secure the support of the ruling party TANU for the continuing expatriate occupation of many senior posts, while at the same time strenuous efforts were made to increase the number of citizens capable of taking over such responsibilities. The situation was, however, fraught with difficulty. Tanzanian Ministers and local officials naturally felt at a serious disadvantage beside the experienced and self-confident expatriate officers, some of whom, while their loyalty to the new disposition was nowhere in question, failed to understand the sensitivities of their new African masters, or to avoid giving an impression of paternalism, which was understandably resented. This impression was compounded by the instinctive caution of many expatriate civil servants, who had a natural penchant for continuity at a time when radical change was inevitable.[7] It is, however, only fair to add that there were also individual expatriate officers whose insight into the changed circumstances enabled them to serve in a manner that was fully supportive of the new leadership,

[4] Cranford Pratt, *The Critical Phase in Tanzania 1945–1968* (Cambridge, 1976), 92.
[5] *Tanzania: Revolution by Education*, ed. Idrian N. Resnick (Arusha, 1968), 6.
[6] Pratt, op. cit. 132.   [7] Pratt, op. cit. 104.

and that close personal friendships resulted, which have stood the test of time.

There is little doubt that at the time of independence the British government expected that Tanganyika would need the services of expatriate officers in government administration for a long time to come and that their presence would help to safeguard the alignment of political and commercial relationships between the two countries. As Iain Macleod said in the House of Commons, 'it is my sincere hope that the great majority of such officers will continue to serve in Tanganyika after it becomes self-governing'.[8] In the event, partly out of consideration for the loss of career prospects and partly in response to localization policy, the great majority of the career officers in the former colonial service withdrew with alacrity, taking advantage of the generous terms offered in compensation for loss of post. The retreat was, indeed, faster than the independent government itself had envisaged and substantial numbers of new expatriate officers had to be recruited on contract, at first overwhelmingly from the United Kingdom, as already seen. But the continuity of colonial policy was broken, if indeed there was any reality in the expectation that it could be safeguarded by the continuing presence of former colonial officers.

The significance of nationality in government service as understood by the British government was not lost on the Tanzanian leadership. In October 1960 Dr Nyerere explained that it was 'the policy of the government that every vacancy arising in the civil service should if possible be filled by an appointment made locally and that recourse should only be had to recruitment from outside East Africa if no suitable candidate of any race could be found locally'. It was, further, 'the government's intention that African candidates of Tanganyika should have prior claim to consideration'.[9] The government was under growing pressure to localize and Nyerere had to make it clear that there were nowhere near enough local people with the training and experience needed to fill the posts currently occupied by the expatriates.

[8] Iain Macleod, Colonial Secretary, Hansard 632, col. 583, 15 Dec. 1960.
[9] Julius Nyerere, speech to the Legislative Council, 19 Oct. 1960.

However, the intensification of pressure from the party persuaded the government to search for new and radical means of accelerating the training and appointment of local candidates. For this they looked for advice, not to their established civil servants, who were in many cases unhappy about what they regarded as dilution and a relaxation of standards, but to the American Ford Foundation. As a result of their advice, Mr David Anderson, an Englishman who had organized a highly successful emergency training scheme in Ghana, was seconded by the Foundation to set in motion a crash training and localization programme.

The deterioration of official relations between Britain and Tanganyika had, however, little to do with the role of the expatriate officers. It was the attitude of the British government towards the government of Ian Smith in Rhodesia that first caused a serious rift between the two countries. The cause of independence in other African countries had already been a matter of active concern with the government party TANU long before independence in Tanganyika. Within the Organization of African Unity the issue was a simple one of self-determination for African majorities and the belief that, in the case of Rhodesia, the British government was more concerned to safeguard the supremacy of white interests. Dr Nyerere insisted that, under the self-government Constitution of 1923 and its successor of 1961, Rhodesia remained in law a British colonial responsibility, and that independence was a matter for Parliament in Westminster. Consequently it was Britain's responsibility to bring about African majority rule.

Relations with Britain first became seriously strained when the Prime Minister Mr Wilson, at a Commonwealth Conference in June 1965, refused a commitment to the denial of Rhodesian independence before the introduction of majority rule—the so-called NIBMAR principle. On 11 November 1965 the Rhodesian government unilaterally declared its independence of Britain. A ministerial meeting of the Organization of African Unity held in Addis Ababa on 2 December thereupon called on all African member states to sever diplomatic relations with Britain on 15 December if Britain as the responsible colonial power had by that date taken no steps to bring down the rebellious government. On 14 December

Nyerere set forth in a speech to the National Assembly in Dar es Salaam the history of Britain's conduct in relation to Rhodesia. He spoke with great moderation. 'Britain's reaction so far', he said, 'has not been encouraging.' But he made abundantly clear what he regarded as Britain's duplicity and self-interest. In seeking the support of the House for a diplomatic breach with Britain, he emphasized that this was a quarrel between governments, not people. British expatriate officers, many of whom were deeply unhappy with their government's conduct, were encouraged to stay and help Tanzania in its hour of need.[10] On the following day diplomatic relations between Britain and Tanzania were broken.[11]

After the breach the Secretary of State for the Colonies announced in the House the suspension of a £7.5 million loan that had been negotiated in support of Tanzania's First Five Year Plan. However, the technical assistance programme and existing commitments for financial aid were to continue, provided that the necessary administrative arrangements could be made.[12] The proposed development loan remained in cold storage until July 1968, when, as will be seen, it was finally cancelled.

Diplomatic relations were resumed on 4 July 1968,[13] ostensibly on the basis of Tanzania's acknowledgement of British commitment to the policy of no independence for Rhodesia without majority rule. But, as Colin Legum observed, 'the resumption of formal links . . . did not significantly change the quality of relations'.[14] In fact, the British government clearly entertained no such commitment and on 22 November 1971, in sole company with South Africa and Portugal, voted against a resolution in the United Nations

---

[10] Julius Nyerere, speech to the National Assembly, 14 Dec. 1965.

[11] Formal relations were also severed by the United Arab Republic, Sudan, Guinea, Algeria, Congo Brazzaville, Mali, and Mauritania.

[12] Anthony Greenwood, Minister for Overseas Development, Hansard 724, written answers to questions, col. 30, 7 Feb. 1966.

[13] George Thomson, Secretary of State for Commonwealth Affairs, Hansard 767, written answers to questions, col. 281, July 1968.

[14] *Africa Contemporary Record 1968–69*, ed. Colin Legum and John Drysdale (London, 1969), article by Colin Legum, p. 22.

Assembly recommending the denial of independence prior to majority rule. But having made their protest in 1965, for Tanzania the rupture no longer served a useful purpose. Tanzania was the last of the African countries that had taken action on the basis of the OAU decision of 2 December 1965 to restore diplomatic relations with Britain and it was obvious that a continued breach by a single African country could have no possible residual protest value.

Resumed diplomatic relations coincided with another cause of friction between the two governments. It had been the practice of the British government to include in the independence settlement with its former colonies an obligation on the newly independent governments to shoulder the cost of pensions and gratuities paid to retired colonial officers. The British government apparently believed that its former colonies would acknowledge their debt for the work of colonial civil servants by accepting this obligation. This unimaginative assumption was no doubt encouraged by the Treasury on financial grounds, but it evoked little echo in Tanzania, where the moral legitimacy of the British mandate was never accepted. For the time being Tanganyika was obliged to accept the British view, but the financial burden became increasingly severe. Britain had eased the passage of this arrangement at independence by a loan of £9 million, but in 1968 repayment was due to begin. In the meantime the recurrent cost of pensions had reached over £1 million. The Tanzanian government therefore proposed an amendment to the Public Officers Agreement which would limit its responsibility to payment in respect of that part of the service of former colonial officers subsequent to independence. When the United Kingdom government refused to accept this arrangement, fearing, no doubt, expensive repercussions in other former colonial territories, the Tanzanian government unilaterally abrogated the Agreement, cutting the necessary budget provision to £130,000 and the acknowledged debt with respect to the compensation loan to £2.5 million.[15] The British government reacted by cancelling the £7.5 million loan still held in cold storage, terminating the recruitment of technical

[15] Amir Jamal, Minister for Finance, budget speech to the National Assembly, 18 June 1968.

assistance staff, and bringing to an end other technical assistance programmes.[16]

Another serious cause of friction was the ambiguous attitude of the British government to the supply of arms to South Africa. In 1963 a Security Council resolution forbade the sale of arms, ammunition, and military vehicles to South Africa. Britain abstained from voting and subsequently announced that it did not consider the ban to be mandatory, or to apply to arms for self-defence, to which South Africa had a right under Article 51 of the United Nations Charter. Further, the British government reserved its position with respect to arms for the defence of the Cape sea route under the Simonstown Agreement with South Africa for the joint use of the Simonstown naval base. In November 1964, with a change of government, a total embargo was imposed, but existing contracts were allowed to continue. However, the incoming Conservative government in 1970 announced an intention to resume sales. The result was a vociferous and sustained protest from most of the African states, while the old Commonwealth countries, especially Canada, denied their support and the United States remained aloof. There was widespread protest inside and outside Parliament.[17] After much hesitation the government announced in February 1972 its readiness to sell arms to South Africa for defence purposes and to honour its obligations under the Simonstown Agreement. Towards the end of 1973 Wasp helicopters were delivered ostensibly for use on South African anti-submarine frigates. On 2 July 1974 a new Labour government restored the embargo on all arms sales and in the following year the Simonstown Agreement was dismantled.

Relations with Britain were also adversely affected by the passage into Tanzanian law in April 1971 of the Act to empower the President to acquire certain Buildings.[18] Those exempted were buildings costing less than shs. 100,000 when

[16] Reginald Prentice, Minister for Overseas Development, Hansard 766, written answers to questions, cols. 175–6, 20 June 1968.

[17] *Africa Contemporary Record 1970–71*, ed. Colin Legum (London, 1971), article by Anthony Hughes, pp. 3–10, *passim*.

[18] An Act to empower the President to acquire certain Buildings: Act No. 13 of 1971.

built (about £5,800) and buildings occupied by their owners for residential, commercial, or industrial purposes. Compensation was payable and based on the original cost of construction and age of the building on a diminishing scale, becoming zero for buildings aged ten years or more. As about £2.5 million of British-owned properties were said to be involved, of which £1.75 million of properties did not qualify for compensation under the Act, protests followed and the British government retaliated by imposing its veto on a proposed £4.3 million World Bank loan in support of peasant tea development.[19] The veto was subsequently lifted at the instance of the Bank.[20] This Act provided a good example of the divergence of political ideas. For the British it involved the defence of the sacred rights of property. For the Tanzanians the intention was to curtail the influence of property rights as instruments of political power and to reduce opportunities for exploitation. Among exploitative landlords excessive rents and such practices as the exaction of key money had become a serious problem.

The Housing Act was one example of a number of departures in policy that were little understood in Europe and caused periodical criticism and hostility in the British Press. Three of these policies deserve mention, as their impact clearly illustrated the insular and unimaginative nature of spontaneous reactions in Britain.

The first example is the policy of non-alignment. On 26 February 1965 Dr Nyerere said, in the course of a speech in the great square in Peking, 'we have . . . determined to adopt a policy of non-alignment in relation to international conflicts that do not concern us. Where there are hostile blocs facing each other on the world stage Tanzania will ignore the threats or blandishments from both sides and pursue her own interests.'[21] This independent posture has often been criticized as unfriendly to the West, but to do so embodies serious misunderstanding. As Dr Nyerere said, 'it really means trying

[19] Anthony Kershaw, Under-Secretary of State for Foreign and Common-wealth Affairs, Hansard 831, written answers to questions, col. 1, 14 Feb. 1972.

[20] *Africa Contemporary Record 1971–72*, ed. Colin Legum (London, 1972), 217 and *African Contemporary Record 1972–73*, 264–5.

[21] Julius Nyerere, speech during a state visit to China.

to be friends with all and not quarrelling with one half of the world in order to seek security with the other half'. However, he well understood the danger of misinterpretation and added, '. . . until the day of independence we in Tanzania were part of one side of an international cold war conflict. In order to tread a middle path on issues that don't concern us, we therefore have to move in a direction towards the other side of that conflict. If you start from a point in the West of the meridian line and want to reach that line, then you have to move East.'[22]

It was in part this movement eastwards towards non-alignment, later reinforced by the government's declared socialist policies, that prompted the unthinking in Britain and America to classify Nyerere's Tanzania as a Marxist state. The stigma of Marxism has been used by some commentators to castigate Tanzania, but these are people who know little about Marx's contribution to political thought and still less about the realities of Tanzania. The fact is that the historical context of Marx's writings bears so little resemblance to the situation in modern Tanzania as to endow much of his thinking with only passing relevance. The danger lies in the use of the time-honoured political terminology of the old world to explain developments in the new. Antithetical ideas like 'capitalism' and 'socialism' fit awkwardly into the structures of Tanzanian life and are best used with caution. 'Free enterprise' certainly exists, is acknowledged, and plays an increasing role, but there is no recognizable *rentier* class and the symptoms of an acquisitive society have been severely limited by a wages policy which has restrained upper-rank incomes in favour of the lower paid. 'Socialism' is the English word used in Tanzania as the equivalent of *ujamaa*, a society built around the relationships and obligations of the family, and has little relevance to the struggles of a Marxian proletariat.

Restraint in trying to fit events in Tanzania into familiar political categories is important not only in the interests of objectivity, but also because Tanzania is groping in her own way towards new solutions to some of the grave underlying

[22] Julius Nyerere, speech at a state banquet during a state visit to the Netherlands, 21 Apr. 1965.

problems that have arisen in our industrial society. Tanzania is aware of such problems as greed, the misuse of economic power, and grave material inequality, which disfigure our own way of life, and is searching for new social structures in which these blemishes have less chance to survive. Ostentatious wealth amidst pervasive poverty is recognized as an obscenity and a socially disruptive influence. Nobody can say whether Tanzania's search for solutions that avoid these pitfalls and enhance social harmony will be successful, but the attempt deserves watchful respect, not critical appraisal in conventional and largely irrelevant political terms.

The third cause of misunderstanding was Tanzania's decision in January 1963 to create a one-party State. It soon became clear that the Westminster model that had guided colonial thinking as the ultimate target in the declining years of the mandate was not to survive as the objective of future development. Already in 1961 Dr Nyerere wrote of his doubts about the suitability for Africa of the Anglo-Saxon form of democracy.[23] Considering that representative government of but the most tentative and partial kind had only been introduced in 1951 and that nothing recognizably similar to the West-minster pattern had been conceded until the constitutional reforms of December 1959, two years before independence, the lack of enthusiasm for Westminster institutions is scarcely surprising. Nevertheless, this has not forestalled criticism of the one-party State as undemocratic and dictatorial in its implications.

All democratic institutions have to be judged by their ability to represent the popular will and their flexible response to changes in public attitudes and opinions. It is not hard to understand that where the electorate is largely illiterate, the Press limited in scope and outreach, the country divided by local or religious loyalties, the force of tradition local rather than nationwide, the institutions of government as we know them are unlikely to produce a popular consensus. As Lord Balfour wrote in his introduction to Bagehot, 'constitutions are easily copied, temperaments are not; and if it should happen that the borrowed constitution and the native

---

[23] Julius Nyerere, from an article in *Africa Speaks* (Princeton, 1961).

temperament fail to correspond, the misfit may have serious results'.[24]

We must leave on one side a judgement as to whether the Tanzanian experiment in one-party government has, or has not, been successful. But two aspects of the Tanzanian example are noteworthy. First, it was carefully and responsibly engineered on the basis of recommendations by a Presidential Commission on the Establishment of a Democratic One-party State.[25] This commission considered their remit with much care and in considerable detail. Subjects such as the rights of the individual and safeguards against an abuse of power commanded close attention, prompted by two important memoranda from President Nyerere. Secondly, two successive revisions of the original Interim Constitution in 1977 and 1985 respectively have extended the representative basis of the system of government, suggesting a pragmatic and evolutionary approach.

There seems little doubt that more changes will be needed in time to come. For one thing, the level of popular literacy has risen dramatically since the Interim Constitution was drawn up in 1965; and for another the spread of education and the growing movement of populations have helped to extend the range of vision from local to national concerns. In the meantime, the complex provisions of the one-party Constitution seem to have provided liberally for change within the system, with numerous sitting members at each election losing their seats to their rivals and even Ministers being put out to grass by popular vote. As alternatives to the Westminster model, the Tanzanian constitutions, in spite of their imperfections, can justifiably claim to be a serious endeavour to accommodate the aspirations of a rapidly developing electorate, while preserving national stability and tranquillity. Life is already much more complex and diverse than at the time of independence and it will be interesting to see what further modifications will be made. Tanzanians must work these out

---

[24] Walter Bagehot, *The English Constitution* (Oxford, 1933), introduction by the Earl of Balfour, p. xxii.
[25] *Report of the Presidential Commission on the Establishment of a Democratic One-party State* (Dar es Salaam, 1965).

for themselves and it is certain that they will not be helped by lectures on Westminster democracy.

It was inevitable that the rosy expectations of 1961 should suffer modification in the light of real events. From the outset the Tanzanians under the leadership of Dr Nyerere saw the liberation of Africa from the remaining vestiges of colonial rule and the 'extension to all African citizens of the requirements of human dignity'[26] as the central goal of foreign policy. Britain too, in a vague sort of way, desired the same goal, but was constantly hamstrung by consideration for its own kith and kin and a chronic inability to believe in the capacity of Africans to manage the affairs of state without protracted preparation. It was not easy for politicians to divest themselves of habits of thought generated by long experience of colonial responsibility, or to face either the pace, or the implications, of the drive towards independence.

The cautious British approach to the Rhodesian problem was the result of a complex interplay of influences, which together account for the appearance of vacillation and inconsistency. Rhodesia was unique in being a self-governing colony under the aegis of the Commonwealth Relations Office, not the Colonial Office, and exercising privileges more akin to those of the self-governing Dominions than to those of any former colony. The residual responsibilities of Britain were largely formal and ceremonial, for in Bagehot's terms the 1923 Constitution largely separated the dignified parts from the efficient parts and left Britain, unless it chose to exercise its reserve powers, in possession of the former. In 1961 the Constitution was revised with parliamentary approval, but embodied few changes in the position of the colonial power. Parliament, of course, had the power to revoke the Constitution as a whole, but such a solution, which would have involved the resumption of direct rule from London, was rejected by the British government. Such a step would have gone back over forty years of Rhodesian self-government and was felt likely to cost the support of those white Rhodesians opposed to Mr Smith's government, whose help might be important in bringing the rebellious government to heel.

---

[26] Julius Nyerere, introduction to *Freedom and Unity* (Oxford, 1966), 22.

Add to the vestigiary constitutional role of the British government the psychology of a people anxious to be rid of its remaining colonial entanglements and hostile to any suggestion of becoming more deeply involved, and the vacillations of British policy become clearer. The unilateral declaration of independence was indeed an act of naked rebellion, but the use of force to reverse it would have caused serious divisions in Parliament and the country. Mr Wilson, who appeared to have faith that economic sanctions would bring the rebellious government rapidly to book, preferred the way of negotiation, and successive governments adhered to the same policy.

It is legitimate to ask why the government of the day found little difficulty in securing popular support for the Falklands campaign, yet made no attempt to adopt a similar solution to the Rhodesian crisis. A charge of racial partiality is only part of the explanation, though there can be little doubt that prejudice exerted a significant influence. But much of the responsibility for Britain's enigmatic response to the Rhodesian crisis must lie in the confused state of opinion in the post-imperial period. Having divested itself of most of its former colonial responsibilities, the British public, after the chastening experience of retreat from power under the pressure of independence movements in so many of its overseas dependent territories, had no stomach for a resumption of direct colonial responsibility in circumstances that promised to give endless trouble. Apathy had taken the place of concern for the integrity of imperial possessions. The Falklands episode, on the other hand, was represented as an attack on British territory, involving the safety of our own kith and kin, and the public reaction, a little jingoistic at times, was in part an answer to a deep-rooted and primitive instinct of defence against a hostile incursion.[27]

It is entirely understandable that British behaviour in the face of the Rhodesian crisis should have aroused such an angry response from the African governments represented at Addis Ababa on 2 December 1965. To them it was indecisive, contradictory, selfish, and hypocritical. The tribulations of the imprisoned African leaders and the intense sufferings of the

[27] See e.g. Robert Ardrey, *The Territorial Imperative* (London, 1969).

African population under the scourge of incipient armed uprising and the rebel government's countermeasures only served to intensify their sense of urgency and their dismay at the British reaction. Their resentment was intensified by their conviction that, as Rhodesia was a British colony, Britain alone—as Mr Wilson fully acknowledged—was responsible for dealing with the problem. As Dr Nyerere said, 'that government may delegate its responsibility if it wishes, but it cannot escape it'.[28]

The decision to break off diplomatic relations with Britain, as has been seen, had serious economic consequences for Tanzania. But the step was taken in the belief that it offered the only available means of expressing Tanzania's anger and revulsion at what it saw as Britain's treacherous inactivity. Not all members of the Organization of African Unity followed suit, and in the end the gesture produced no practical effect. But at the time the breach seemed unavoidable in the interests of Tanzania's self-respect.

From this painful episode in Anglo-Tanzanian relations a number of lessons may be learned. The first lesson lies in the importance of understanding the intellectual and emotional force of the African demand for majority government. The impulse for this demand lies not, as some would insultingly claim, in mere power hunger, but in a deep-rooted longing for respect as equal human beings. On this issue Africans are naturally sensitive, for colonial rule, however benign, was based on distinctions of colour and an affront to human dignity. We in Britain do not understand how intense is this feeling among Africans, nor how profoundly they are affected by the servile condition of their brothers in South Africa. On the other hand, it is doubtful whether the confused public reaction in Britain to its post-colonial role is correctly assessed in Tanzania.

The problem here exposed affects a wide range of international relationships. There is a Swahili proverb which runs, 'asiyekujua hakuthamini', or 'he who does not know you does not value you'. The poison that so often sours international relations is ignorance, and a failure to make the imaginative

---

[28] Julius Nyerere, speech to the National Assembly, 14 Dec. 1965.

effort needed to understand the motives that underlie human attitudes and behaviour. The motives are not always pure. Selfishness, power seeking, and false pride abound. But so also do human concern, generosity, and a forgiving spirit. If our anxiety on behalf of our own kith and kin in the Falklands or elsewhere is not altogether ignoble, neither is the concern of our Tanzanian friends for their 'kith and kin' in South Africa. To be willing and able to enter into each other's worries and concerns is surely the solvent of many misunderstandings.

But in the way of understanding stands one serious difficulty. We are prone to judge one another by our own standards. It is indeed difficult to do otherwise. Yet the greater the mutual knowledge the more aware do we become of each other's frame of reference and the more readily are we able to form judgements on that basis. An example of this problem can be found in the respect that we pay to efficiency. Notwithstanding our own many lapses from grace, we worship efficiency as an essential ingredient of an orderly, civilized life and we are apt to deplore in a spirit of superiority the inefficiencies so evident in Tanzania and elsewhere. Efficiency is important, for Tanzania as well as ourselves, as the Tanzanian leadership fully realizes. But there are circumstances under which Tanzanians value unity of purpose more highly. Anyone who has endured what to us seem endless, time-wasting discussions on matters requiring decision will have come to realize that achieving a common mind is seen in Tanzania as having greater importance than the prompt dispatch of business. In a phrase from Guy Clutton-Brock describing a meeting of elders, which Nyerere quotes with approval, 'they talk till they agree'.[29] Efficiency as we know it takes second place.

It is, moreover, necessary to realize that Tanzania does not yet have a trained and disciplined work-force such as we have developed over many years of gradual growth since the days of the Industrial Revolution. The background of many urban dwellers is the countryside, where widespread adult literacy is a recent development and where the habit of regulating the working day by the clock remains largely unknown to this day.

[29] Julius Nyerere, from an article in *Africa Speaks* (Princeton, 1961).

We must also remember that Tanzania is a country undergoing rapid change. The population has increased by 120 per cent since independence to a total of over 23 million. By 1984 the primary-school population had risen by 630 per cent to over 3½ million. Rural dispensaries have increased in number from 990 at independence to 2,831 today, a growth of 186 per cent. Electricity consumption had gone up from 166 to 785 million kilowatt hours by 1985, or 370 per cent.[30] These changes have been accompanied by changes in thought and outlook. The institutional expression of Tanzania's underlying philosophy of socialism and self-reliance enunciated in the Arusha Declaration of 1967 has been modified in the light of experience. Life is becoming more ramified, expectations more diverse. Clearly any static assessment of Tanzania will not do.

The relations between governments are only one aspect of relations between countries. Intergovernmental relations are affected by strategic and commercial considerations and formal international obligations of a kind that often have little meaning for individuals in their relations one with another. Governmental attitudes are not a simple reflection of ideological preferences. The breach in relations to which reference has been made took place during a Labour administration in Britain, which one would have thought sympathetic to the socialist aspirations of the Tanzanian government and party. Throughout the premiership of Mr Wilson the Tanzanians found the attitude of the British government most disturbing. There is in fact an underlying continuity in government attitudes that is superimposed on the particular policies of successive governments and has more to do with the public mood than with any immediate political calculation.

It is because of the influence of perceived public attitudes on the assumptions underlying official policies that the educational endeavours of non-governmental bodies are so important. Such work is unlikely to penetrate fully into the legal, financial, diplomatic, and strategic niceties that are considered during the formation of government policies, but it can create a disposition towards friendly relationships and

[30] *Hali ya Uchumi wa Taifa katika Mwaka 1971 and 1985* (Dar es Salaam, 1972 and 1986).

greater mutual understanding. The work of the voluntary bodies is distinctive in that it originates in personal relations and benefits from the many insights that are the result of such human contacts. It is this special feature that equips the voluntary bodies to cultivate relationships of a more fundamental and enduring kind than the official posture of governments would sometimes imply.

One aspect of intergovernmental relations must not be forgotten. It has to do with the formal relations between two nation states. President Nyerere was aware that in his own country and almost within his own lifetime local and family loyalties had gradually extended their reach; but at independence nation-building was far from complete and much thought was given by the new government to the means of consolidating a sense of nationhood. However, Dr Nyerere saw the nation as an intermediate stage in world development. 'With the irresistible force of a glacier inching down to the sea, the movement towards greater human contact has continued since the world began.' In his Dag Hammarskjöld Lecture he made a plea for practical co-operation, which later became the philosophical basis for the Tanzanian policy of *ujamaa*. 'Cooperation and conflict', he claimed, 'are two sides of the same coin; both arise out of man's relationship with his fellows.' Believing that 'there must exist a focus of loyalty beyond the nation state',[31] he argued on behalf of progress towards the creation of a supranational authority to preside over world unity.

The form and function of that ultimate supranational body are still obscured from view, but work on the foundations has begun. It is concerned with 'man's relationship with his fellows', with positive measures to encourage growth in mutual understanding, mutual respect, and a quickened sense of a common humanity. Lord Robert Cecil once spoke of 'that hoary old humbug—si pacem vis para bellum'. He was right. Whatever may be claimed for the balance of terror in the last quarter century, it has left unresolved a spirit of hostility buttressed by insults and gross misrepresentations. There is no substitute for true knowledge, understanding, and respect if true peace is to be achieved and preserved.

[31] Julius Nyerere, Dag Hammarskjöld Memorial Lecture, 23 Jan. 1964.

From Command to Service: Trevor Huddleston in Masasi, 1960–1968

TERENCE RANGER

WHEN I first went to Southern Africa in 1957, ill equipped by six years of an Oxford education, Trevor Huddleston's *Naught for Your Comfort* was the only book about Africa I had read. Six years later, rather better equipped by means of participation in the black nationalist parties of what was then Southern Rhodesia, I was deported from that country. I found myself Professor of History at the new University College of Dar es Salaam. Much though I enjoyed the experience of living in independent rather than colonial Africa, it was hard to move from the intense excitement and involvement with Africans in the Zimbabwean nationalist struggle to the quite different tasks which confronted a white expatriate professional in an African nation. It was a comfort to me to know that Trevor Huddleston had made that same transition—from the turmoil of the South African black townships to the diocese of Masasi, in Tanzania's sleepy and impoverished south-east. I promised myself that I would seek to learn from him how to manage this transition.

In the years that followed I did indeed have the opportunity to learn from him. He came to talk to my students at the university about the positive values of poverty, or at least of moderation. I twice visited Masasi. These visits were important to me in many ways. They gave me some vivid memories—of Bishop Huddleston crossing the cathedral yard surrounded by minute African children; of his retreat to his house for prayer and meditation, followed immediately by the sound within of the unmeditative call-sign of Radio South Africa as he caught up with recent events there; of the intense interactions of local Anglicans and Catholics in the aftermath of the Vatican Council. Visiting Masasi made me conscious of the realities of poverty and the difficulties of development. It also unexpectedly channelled and directed my historical research.

Trevor Huddleston had collected together the parish diaries from all over the diocese in order to preserve them from damp and red ants. He entrusted them to me for delivery to the University Library; I began to read them and discovered an extraordinary source for social history. Over the next few years I came to learn a good deal about Masasi and particularly about the nature of the Anglican tradition which Huddleston inherited when he became bishop there in 1960. And then in 1975 a field research visit to Masasi seven years after his depature led to the discovery of documents about his own episcopate. I had been asking Huddleston's successor as bishop, Hilary Chisonga, whether there were any historical records at the cathedral and he had been telling me that none survived except the slimmest of files about the founding days of the late nineteenth century. At length, to satisfy my persistent curiosity, he good-naturedly told me to go and look in the store, where there might be papers. And so there were, strewn all over the floor under the bags of meal and the grass-cutters: thousands of files on the diocesan school system and on Huddleston's surrender of these schools to the local authorities in 1967.

I knew that these papers were not thought of as 'historical' —after all my visit took place only eight years after the surrender. I also knew that the hard-pressed Church could not spare the time or money to employ someone to go through them or to set up an archive. I doubted that they would long survive. It was my last day in Masasi. So I spent a hectic ten hours grasping at the most significant documents and noting them, so that there would be some record of this significant transition for the Church.

I have barely looked at my notes on these files since then, but the editor's request for a contribution to this volume has taken me back to them. Reading through them, I have come to understand much better the nature of the task which faced

Huddleston in Masasi in the 1960s; the nature of the Anglican Church's transition, as he himself expressed it in 1967, from management or command to service.

In what follows, then, I intend to draw partly on my memory, partly on letters written to me at the time from and about Masasi, and largely on this education archive. It is, I am afraid, all too typical of the academic historian thus to turn the pleasures of reminiscence into the aridities of archival research. I hope, though, that the method may throw some light on one of the less dramatic but one of the most important periods of Trevor Huddleston's career.

I begin by drawing on two letters from my own correspondence files for the 1960s. The first shows how the contrast between Sophiatown and Masasi struck some experienced international observers. In 1965 the BBC sent a television team to Tanzania to make two documentaries, one on a 'black statesman', Julius Nyerere, and the other on a 'white missionary', Trevor Huddleston. I had met the leader of this team in Southern Rhodesia when he was making a radio programme about the nationalist protest marches and demonstrations of 1960. I had last seen him in the thick of the agitated townships of Salisbury. He admired Huddleston as a man who had lived among and triumphantly expressed the atmosphere of township vitality. Off he went with his cameramen to interview and film Huddleston in Masasi. He found it a baffling experience. Instead of an activist priest, sharing urban poverty with his politically aroused flock, he found a High Anglican bishop, presiding in full regalia over elaborate ceremonials in what seemed an incongruously vast cathedral. My reporter friend could not see the relevance of this sort of church to the needs of Masasi district, which he himself expressed in terms of 'development'. He thought Huddleston too much concerned about the problems of this church and not enough concerned with development.

He poured out all this perplexity and disillusionment to me on his return to Dar es Salaam. The letter from him which survives in my files, dated 27 October 1965, was in fact written in a more positive mood after a second visit to Masasi, but it still speaks clearly enough of the contrasts which he drew between church concerns and the interests of the people: 'I came away from my second visit there a little less pessimistic about the Bishop, in one particular. I think he really does still have the energy to drive for socio-economic development *as such* and almost in spite of his Church responsibilities.'

The second letter from my files was written in a very different mood and by a very different correspondent. It came from a young American Catholic nun, recently posted to Masasi, who greatly admired Huddleston as a true bishop and leader of the universal Church. In March 1967 she visited him to share her own anxieties about ecclesiastical institutions. Her letter reveals something of Huddleston's own vision of the ideal response in a situation in which expatriate leadership and spokesmanship seemed increasingly beside the point:

We talked about Milwaukee and Masasi. He experiences many of the same things that I do in our work of witnessing Christ in and around Masasi. I am very much struck by his simplicity. He told me that when he was 21 he read a life of Charles Foucauld and then travelled to the Holy Land and visited all the places Charles had stayed at during that period of his life. He feels Foucauld's way of life, the simple 'presence among' people, is the best way of getting the gospel message across to the people here.

Reading both these letters now I am struck by their Utopianism. For my BBC friend, 'development' was a good which should be striven for irrespective of structures. The American nun longed 'to be just an ordinary villager, living as the people do in and around this place'. Neither really responded to the specific history of Masasi, and of the Church in Masasi, a history which conditioned both what Huddleston could do and what he had to do.

The Universities' Mission to Central Africa (UMCA), which had founded Masasi nearly a century earlier, had long combined radicalism and High Churchmanship, a life among villagers and aspirations to development, in a way calculated to bewilder television reporters and modern nuns alike. Masasi cathedral was in fact a legacy of the UMCA's initial triumphalist stage, when an Anglican theology/sociology expected to found towns as the capital cities of tribal nations in southern Tanzania. The building was very untypical of the way in which the UMCA's work had actually developed.

The missionaries had soon discovered that south-east Tanzania was a country of ethnic fragments and of small, shifting settlements. Disillusioned with its alliance with so-called 'kings' and 'chiefs', the UMCA settled down to become a village church—or rather a church of transitory hamlets. Its clergy houses, schools, and clinics were famous—or notorious —for their simplicity. In a real sense, UMCA teachers and clergy *had* been a 'presence among' the people. Indeed, one of the tensions of the early independence period was that, while expatriate observers wanted the Church to live 'as the people', many Tanzanians regarded the simplicity of UMCA schools and teachers' houses as inappropriate to a proud new nation:

As far as I can see [wrote P. S. Nhigula, Regional Education Officer, to Trevor Huddleston on 1 November 1965], your schools in Newala are faced with:

(*a*) The low quality of school buildings, including teachers' quarters.
(*b*) The delay in payment of teachers' salaries.
(*c*) Inadequate provision of school equipment and materials.

I hope your Education Secretary will try his best to put things right, though of course this cannot be done overnight.

Huddleston himself believed that other improvements were even more urgently necessary. As he told a group of senior African teachers, seeking his support for improved conditions in April 1961, he had discovered soon after his appointment as bishop that:

The clergy of the Masasi diocese were being paid a salary which is a positive disgrace to the Church . . . There is no priest of this diocese, of however great seniority, who receives a salary comparable to that of our teachers. There are many of them who receive little more than the pay of a labourer . . . Nearly all of them are in need of better housing.

Yet if the past record of the UMCA in south-east Tanzania had been one of what now appeared excessive simplicity, it certainly had also been one of development. Huddleston correctly replied in 1966 to critics of church schools that, 'in the field of Primary Education in this Region, we, as an

Agency, have nothing to be ashamed of. On the contrary it is true to say that without the initiative and sacrifice of the Benedictine Fathers and UMCA there would be no education here today at all.' The village school had been the major means of missionary expansion in south-east Tanzania and there had, indeed, been intense competition between Anglicans and Catholics. The UMCA were famous for seeking to adapt these schools to indigenous values and in particular for having Christianized the boys' initiation ceremonies and co-ordinated these with progress in church and school life. The result was a widely literate agrarian society. As Huddleston told the assembled teachers of the diocese in April 1967, 'we have nothing to be ashamed of in our educational effort: one day it will be known for what it is, even if, at present it is little thought of—or thought of as a relic of colonialism'.

This combination of village education and agricultural production *did* later on come to be praised by Julius Nyerere as a forerunner of his own educational philosophy. But in the early 1960s the UMCA tradition had gone out of fashion; its schools and hospitals and salaries seemed much too simple and its notions of development lop-sided. On the eve of independence numerous resentments swirled around south-east Tanzania. Muslims resented the long dominance by Catholics and Anglicans of all educational provision in the region. Christian progressives, who had gone on to secondary and even professional training out of the relatively strong regional primary-school network, resented the lack of openings for advancement in their home area. As the District Commissioner, Masasi, reported in 1955:

One of the main problems facing the people of Masasi District [is] that although they enjoy a high level of education the only livelihood open to the majority of them is in agriculture . . . very many of the boys now studying in the District's Secondary, Middle and Primary Schools must inevitably look to farming as their career. . . . A certain growth of anti-Mission feeling was also noticeable originating perhaps from a realisation that the Missions have had too big a say in the running of the Districts affairs in the past by virtue of their complete monopoly of almost all the social services. (Annual Report, Masasi District, 1955, file 306/R3/2, National Archives, Dar es Salaam.)

The dilemma of the Anglican Church with the coming of

independence was that Tanzanian authorities—local authorities, regional bureaucrats, central government—wanted to assert more and more control over areas which had once been the monopoly of the Church, such as education. At the same time, however, the central government did not wish the voluntary agencies to withdraw altogether from educational provision and management, judging that the local authorities lacked both administrative experience and financial resources. Hence in Masasi diocese the Church found itself tied to the task of managing a network of primary schools which no longer served their old purpose as focuses of the Christian community. Inevitably Anglican management of these schools attracted a barrage of criticism from local authorities who aspired to take over the whole system; inevitably, also, the Church resented both the criticism and the failure by local authorities to remit the money due from them for the support of church schools. Once their schools had been a source of influence and popularity. Now they had become a cause of bitterness and ill-feeling, setting the Church against the local representatives of the new Tanzania. To be free to engage in what mý BBC friend thought of as 'rural development', to be free to become a simple presence among the people, even to be free to engage constructively with the aspirations of independence, the Church had to disentangle itself from these old commitments.

A further difficulty of what can be thought of as this 'transitional' period of independence, before the proclamation of the Arusha Declaration and of 'Education for Self-Reliance' in 1967, was that the Tanzanian government itself was unclear about its development priorities. It knew that it wanted to modernize and to enrich, but in these years it was not sure how to modernize and who to enrich. It was patriotic duty, as well as self-interest, for Tanzanian teachers to demand to be paid as well as expatriates, and for voluntary-agency teachers to demand the same terms and pensions as teachers employed by the State. The churches might have their private reservations—'It may be argued that the Civil Service terms were originally devised to attract Europeans to "backward" and "dangerous" countries', wrote the Education Secretary-General of the Christian Council of Tanganyika, 'and hence the paternal paraphernalia of free pension, subsidized housing, free medical treatment, etc. Is it right, either on grounds of general policy or sound economy, to go on extending these privileges more widely to the nationals of the territory?' But in public there was no choice but to support church teachers in their demand for a unified teaching service in which all shared these privileges.

Once again, however, the new Tanzanian government was reluctant to move rapidly because of the great cost of a unified service. It was not until 1965 that a unified teaching service came into existence, after much teacher militancy and protest. Inevitably a good deal of this was directed against the churches. 'Too often our teachers show a hostility to religion', wrote the Bishop of South-west Tanganyika, 'perhaps as a means of asserting their independence.' Huddleston was immediately bombarded with teacher petitions when he arrived in Masasi late in 1960. When I first wrote to him to ask that he come to speak to my students on 'positive poverty' he replied that it would be impossible in such a climate to make them understand what he was talking about.

The American nun, having reported Huddleston's Foucauld-style vision, went on to write:

I agree, but I don't know if it is possible right now. We are very far from identifying that completely. I am finding my teaching to be a very exacting and intriguing work—but not really intimately Gospel witnessing, mainly due to the fact that a school is a school, kind of set apart from the more homely affairs of usual family living. I keep wanting just to be an ordinary villager. This desire may be just an 'always wish', for our commitment to this school is going to be a lengthy one.

Huddleston's main task in Masasi was to ensure that a vision of egalitarian 'socio-economic development', arising out of the involvement of the Church with the people, did not remain just an 'always wish'. Among much else, this involved ensuring that commitment to the schools was not *too* lengthy.

I hope that I have now set the context for a discussion of the story which emerges from the education papers I found in the store-shed at Masasi. At first sight it is a tedious story, narrowly focused on 'church responsibilities', and light years away from the drama of the South African townships. At second reading, though, it is the story of a necessary emancipation. This freeing of the Church was made possible partly by Huddleston's personal qualities and partly by the ending of Tanzania's uncertainties about development objectives with the publication of the Arusha documents in 1967. Huddleston's policies, which had led to many clashes with local officials in the years before 1967, ended up magnificently in harmony with the ideals of *ujamaa*. After the Arusha Declaration he wrote to me to say that he now *could* talk to my students about honest and holy poverty. After the Arusha Declaration, too, the Church in Masasi could move towards an up-dated version of its old commitment to simple self-development.

It seems clear that Huddleston was nominated as Bishop of Masasi because it was felt that his record in South Africa qualified him to work with the authorities of a newly independent African state. One of the first letters I noted in the Masasi store-shed, written in April 1960 from one missionary to another, expressed the fear that Huddleston might be vetoed by the Archbishop of Canterbury because of his radicalism—because 'he had disapproved of apartheid'— and the hope that he would nevertheless be appointed 'to restore confidence all round during the doubtless trying days of the beginning of *uhuru* (independence)'. But if the local clergy had hoped to find merely a conciliator in Huddleston they had miscalculated. In August 1975 I talked with old Canon Donald Parsons, then in retirement in Mtwara. He ranged over all the bishops of Masasi with whom he had worked, characterizing each with a brisk few words. Huddleston, he said, had been 'flamboyant, kind and not patient'.

And indeed there *is* plenty of evidence of impatience in the files from the Masasi store-room, though it seems to me to have been a necessary and salutary impatience. Huddleston was impatient with the frustrating limitations on the freedom of action of the Church; he was frank in his response to demands and criticisms; and once he had decided that the surrender of the church schools was the only remedy he drove towards that end. The very first letter by Huddleston which I found at Masasi reveals his style. In April 1961 he received

two representations from teachers, one deploring housing
conditions, salaries, lack of promotion chances, and so on; the
other asking that school supervisors be provided with motor
cycles. 'We teachers not to blame the voluntary agencies for
failure to keep proper conditions of service parallel to those of
the civil servants', wrote Stephen Salileje on 26 April. 'They
could do all in a small scale but not in a large scale as it is
now.' Huddleston's reply was frank in its statement of his
priorities:

At least £1000 would be required for the purchase of the bicycles and
I had to discover where—if anywhere—this money could be found.
What in fact I *did* discover was that the Education Dept., so far from
having money available, had such an enormous and crippling debt
that the whole diocese was suffering in consequence . . . At the same
time I discovered that the clergy of the Masasi diocese were being
paid a salary which is a positive disgrace to the Church . . . There is
no priest in this diocese—of however great seniority—who receives a
salary comparable to that of our teachers. . . . Taking these two facts
together . . . my first duty as bishop of Masasi is absolutely clear. It
is to eliminate the debt and to reorganise the whole financial structure
of the diocese . . .

   I have every sympathy with your request. I recognise absolutely
that it is unfair to expect our supervisors to do their job without
adequate transport. I think it most undesirable that there should be
such a distinction between Government and Mission Schools. (Indeed
I will do all I can to work for a unified system) . . . [but] I ask you to
recognise that the claim of the priests, deacons and catechists to a
living wage must be met *before any other is considered*. This, at least, is
my own firm conviction and policy.

He was as frank in response to another demand. In June 1962
P. Mwidadi, Chairman of the Masasi branch of the National
Union of Teachers wrote to press for more rapid Africanization
of the church educational system. Huddleston set out the
African promotions and appointments that were taking place,
but added:

I think it is essential that I should stress the point that in this Diocese
because we are attempting to run our institutions on Christian lines,
I am determined to keep our multi-racial character so far as possible
in evidence. The Christian Church cannot compromise with racialism
of any kind and it would be a defeat for this principle if I were to

allow the very necessary and immediate need for Africanisation to lead to a false balance.

In July 1964 the newly appointed diocesan education secretary J. A. Majiyapwani circulated all the church teachers with a memorandum on the disciplinary code, in which he warned women teachers that 'having an illegitimate baby is immoral conduct and is disgracing the teaching profession'. Huddleston at once responded by telling Majiyapwani that this was not true.

The immoral conduct is *the act of extra-marital sexual intercourse* . . . Men-teachers are just as guilty as women-teachers if they commit such acts. I would be grateful if the male members of the teaching profession could be urged to recognise their own responsibility for maintaining the Code of Professional Conduct. In my experience, they need this reminder at least as much as and probably more than the women.

Huddleston's note went to all teachers.

It is clear, then, that he held the line against pressure from increasingly articulate male teachers. This did little to soothe teacher resentments, which were mainly caused by the great delays in the implementation of the unified service, but in each case it seems to me to have been a line necessary to have held. In his comments on the local authorities of the south-east, however, frankness often gives way to impatience. In July 1963 he wrote to the Regional Commissioner about the failure of Tunduru District Council to pay the subventions it owed to the church school at Mindu, describing the resulting situation as 'immoral, and indeed impossible', and demanding that government compel the Council to meet its obligations. Similar failures by District Councils continued and indeed increased over the next two years, driving the church education office to more and more desperate shifts. By September 1965 Huddleston's patience with the local authorities had been exhausted.

On 29 September the Newala District Education Committee met. Its Executive Officer S. T. Nathan criticized the state of the Anglican primary schools; alleged that money given by the District Council for their maintenance and equipment had not been properly accounted for; and announced that 'the District

Council intended to take over [the] schools as soon as possible'. Nathan then sent to Huddleston the agenda for a meeting on 8 October, indicating that he should attend to discuss this take-over. Huddleston exploded. He was soon to conclude that the only solution lay in surrendering all church schools but he was not prepared to tolerate Newala's action:

I have no intention of handing over our Lower Primary Schools to the District Council without a full and thorough consultation in terms of the Education Ordinance [he wrote to the Regional Education Officer, Mhigula, on 7 October]. I have no intention of accepting the orders of one District Council in a matter of such importance. . . .
I am surprised at the attitude of the Executive Officer towards this Agency. I am certainly not prepared to accept his criticisms and accusation without having the opportunity to answer them.

On 5 November he wrote again to say that the Executive Officer, Newala, 'seems to think that it is my duty to attend meetings'; that he was 'exceeding his authority in summoning me'; and that 'if there is any further trouble of this kind, I fear I shall have to refer the matter directly to Dar es Salaam'. When the Regional Education Officer tactfully suggested that a meeting be held at Masasi to sort out the issue, Executive Officer Nathan riposted that Huddleston had no right to summon *him*!

By January 1966 the same tensions had arisen between Huddleston and the Masasi District Education Committee, which had decided to take over direct responsibility for feeding boarders in church upper primary boarding schools. Huddleston insisted that 'so long as we are the controlling agency we must have the right to control the feeding of the children in our schools . . . I am not prepared to hand over this responsibility to the Council.' In this instance the vigour of Huddleston's complaints ruffled the Masasi District Education Officer, ex-UMCA teacher George Kasembe.

It was plain that the school issue was seriously straining relations between the Church and local government. George Kasembe's own account of the controversy in Masasi makes it plain also that by this time Huddleston's mind was turning to the ideal of giving up the schools so as to concentrate on other development projects:

The Bishop says that this taking over feeding of Voluntary Agency Upper Primary Schools should never be done without consulting him, he is not content, as this shows clearly that the control of his schools has been taken away from him. 'I don't mind', he said, 'if control of schools be taken over by the Local Authority, the Local Authority may do so at any time. What I mind is that the taking over be done by following proper channels, e.g. openly and in writing, not obscurely. I shall be glad' the Bishop continued, 'to spend my money in other similar ways, e.g. helping the handicapped children, etc.'

From this time on Huddleston increasingly stressed the higher priority which he gave to the other development projects of the Church. Thus in September 1966 he replied to a request from the Executive Officer of Masasi District Council for money to improve teachers' houses by spelling out that over the past two years the Church had spent £75,000 on improving and extending its main hospital, building three new dispensaries, building and equipping an agricultural school, and providing a plough and tractor for a local farming co-operative:

The time has come to use our resources where they will be of most value. And it is impossible for us to help in every area of development at once. . . . As the control of these schools is already virtually in the hands of the Local Authority—which collects its funds through taxation of the whole community—it is not unreasonable that the provision of adequate housing should rest also with the Local Authority. But whether it does or not, there is no possibility whatever of my Agency accepting this as a priority in Nation-building at this time.

By the end of 1966 Huddleston longed to be free of the schools altogether. January 1967 saw the coincidence of two events, one national and the other very local. The local event was the failure of Masasi District Council to pay teachers' salaries in church schools; the national event was the Arusha Declaration, which emphasized that Tanzanians ought to be self-reliant and not to depend on outside aid. Huddleston decided that the time had come to make both local and central government face up to their responsibilities. He gave notice that he would not advance money to meet teachers' salaries in Masasi District after the end of January. If local resources, supplemented by grants from Dar es Salaam, could not support so many schools they would have to close. This precipitated a hasty visit from S. A. Nalitolela from the Ministry of Education in Dar es Salaam, who managed to patch together a compromise to keep the Masasi schools open without a great increase in state subvention. But Huddleston made clear to Nalitolela that 'Education was primarily the responsibility of the State and the sooner the State took over all of this responsibility the better. He was not prepared to spend money on Primary Schools because his priorities were extensions to Hospital buildings and provision of decent houses to clergy.'

In March, when funding from Tunduru District Council failed, he was still reluctantly accepting the burden of the schools:

I personally have no desire to continue with the management of schools and feel that it is a quite disastrous waste of time and money, but I am prepared to go on if, by doing so, I can help the development of this part of the country. Certainly I am not going on because of any advantage to myself or the Diocese.

By April, however, Nyerere's statement on Education for Self Reliance was published, with its emphasis on egalitarianism, the integration of education into rural society, a commitment to agricultural production, and an emphasis on self-reliance. This forceful restatement of the ideals of the UMCA tradition decided Huddleston that the time had come to bring an end to the farce. On 1 April he wrote to Nalitolela:

I am calling a meeting of all my teachers on April 15th to discuss the future of all our schools . . . I shall press very strongly that we hand over control of virtually all our Primary Schools at the earliest possible moment. I feel that this is in line with virtually all that the President himself has said with regard to education policy, and that it is much more likely that the local community will bestir itself and take responsibility if it is no longer possible to rely on the voluntary agency.

In a pamphlet *The State of Anglo-Tanzanian Relations*, published by the Africa Bureau, Huddleston later set out what the Arusha Declaration had meant to him. The Declaration brought 'idealism right into the political arena within

Tanzania'; everyone in office in State or party had to give up capitalist aspirations; at the level of the peasant farmer it meant 'more popular participation in development plans that are the real expression of African socialism'. All these things were 'linked very closely with the new emphasis on Self-Reliance'.

In this pamphlet Huddleston quoted the Declaration on self-reliance. He added:

On the radio, on posters and stickers the slogan 'USIWE KUPE—JITEGEMEE' is widely propagated. It means literally 'Don't be a parasite—be self-reliant.' Even the smallest child in a primary school will chuckle if you use this phrase when he asks you for a lift in your car or a few cents for sweets!

On 15 April 1967 he cited the same passage of the Declaration not to primary-school children but to their teachers, in a long address which began with a text from St Matthew and ended with one from Nyerere. He placed the issue of schools before them, asking for a vote which would influence the decision of synod. He recommended the immediate surrender of schools without any delay. The existing system was unworkable: 'The Teacher is employed by two masters: paid by one (Government/Local Authority); moved, promoted or demoted by the other (Voluntary Agency); (housed by whom?). And in case of conflict or difficulty, to which authority must he turn?' Moreover, it was a drain on resources: 'Our President pointed out in his statement on "Education for Self-Reliance" that 20% of the country's budget was being spent on Education and that this was really more than the country could afford.' The diocese had been spending at least as high a proportion of its funds and 'we are neglecting our duty in other, more urgent, needs'.

Huddleston then laid down a programme for the Church once freed of the schools:

It can no longer be said that a Voluntary Agency School is necessarily a Christian school at all. It is quite possible that half its staff may now be Muslim and 90% of its children. This is not a bad thing and I do not criticise it at all. The Government must provide for ALL, not Christians only. But the fact is that our main task as a Diocese is to proclaim the Gospel of Christ and to care for the Christian community.

. . . It is no longer honest to say that our Primary Schools are either centres of evangelisation, or in themselves, Christian institutions. But there are great areas of need which the Church is neglecting because it is using its resources of men and money in this way . . . The training of lay evangelists. The encouragement of agricultural development. The care of the handicapped. All that is known as 'Works of Mercy,' and that ought to be the *first* concern of the Church, we are hardly touching.

He ended by stressing the Arusha call to be 'self-reliant in every possible way', declaring that as 'Bishop of Masasi I want every Christian in the diocese to take these words to heart—and to ACT upon them'.

The teachers overwhelmingly supported the motion to surrender the schools. Huddleston then summoned a diocesan synod for July 1967, telling Nalitolela in the Ministry of Education that he was by no means sure how synod would decide but that, if it went against his recommendation, 'I would have to reconsider my position as Bishop'. There was no need for this. Synod accepted his resolution, voting to surrender the schools and to offer financial assistance to the Local Authorities for a further three years so as to assist their administration of them. 'The Church is here to *serve* in any way it can', said Huddleston, 'but no longer to *manage* or govern . . . This, as I see it, is the logical consequence of the Arusha Declaration.' In October the Ministry of Education agreed that the handover should be effected throughout the districts of the Masasi diocese as from 1 November.

The way was open for a Church of service, a Church which might combine the 'agricultural development' which my BBC friend wanted and which Huddleston called for in his speech to the teachers with the 'Works of Mercy' which were so close to the heart of the Masasi American nun. In Tanzania as a whole the edgy ambiguities of the period of transition were giving way to the moral certainties of the Arusha Declaration of which Huddleston so much approved. Yet we shall never know how he might have developed his ministry in these new and more favourable circumstances because he resigned as bishop even while the church schools were still being handed over and left Tanzania early in 1968. He did this in the logic of the gospel of self-reliance, believing that the time had come for

a Tanzanian bishop of Masasi. It was left to his successor
Hilary Chisonga to see what could be done without schools to
run and in the Tanzania of the Arusha Declaration.

I have omitted a great deal of what was important in Trevor
Huddleston's time in Tanzania. I have said nothing of his
close relations with Roman Catholics in south-east Tanzania,
nor of his courageous complaints to central government
whenever he came across arbitrary or brutal official action.
The unglamorous activities I *have* concentrated on seem to me
to have been of the essence, however—things that had to be
done, no matter how much they took away from the things he
wanted to do. As I read through these papers now it makes me
reflect on my own time in Tanzania and to wonder whether I
managed to defend the rights and to open up the opportunities
of the academic 'church' with as much frankness and justified
impatience.

In the same logic of self-reliance, and partly as a result of
conversations with Huddleston, I also resigned my position to
make way for a Tanzanian successor. I left the country in 1969
as full of hope for its future as was Huddleston in 1968. But I
must conclude this chapter with a brief statement of the ironies
which subsequent events revealed in both our positions. In
1975 when I revisited Masasi—and found the storehouse
papers—I saw and heard for myself some of the consequences
of the Arusha Declaration. Shortly before there had been
enforced 'villagization' throughout the south-east; the multi-
plicity of hamlets had been replaced by forty or fifty large
rural 'towns'. This was the result of a loss of patience on a
grander and more damaging scale than anything displayed by
Huddleston. 'Popular participation in development plans'
had not had rapid enough results so it gave way to social
engineering from the top. It wasn't what Huddleston had
looked forward to and the clergy, both black and white, to
whom I talked in 1975 universally deplored it. It had
destroyed the old communal context of church life and action.
Worse than that, it had destroyed confidence in 'self-reliance'.

In December 1986 I was invited to a conference in Arusha
on the Declaration twenty years later. The young Tanzanian
academics who dominated the conference with their eloquence

and humour frequently used the term 'commandism' to describe authoritarian government action since 1975. They found it hard to understand how Huddleston and I and so many others had seen in the Declaration the promise of true participatory development. They were more inclined to praise resistances to the encroachment of state power than surrenders of authority to the State. In this they were being false historians just as we had been false prophets. Perhaps it was always unrealistic to look forward to a State of service as well as to a Church of service. Certainly if Huddleston had stayed on in Masasi he would have found himself in a very different environment from the one he anticipated. Yet I am sure he would have found a way to speak for participatory self-reliant development in the late 1970s, just as despite all the failures of the Arusha Declaration it needs to be spoken for today, not as an exploded illusion but as an essential for Tanzanian society and for the Tanzanian Church.

A Tale of Two Streets:
Cable Street, Brick Lane,
and Organized Racism

KENNETH LEECH

IN 1958 Trevor Huddleston was just past the peak of his fame as far as the British public was concerned. The return from South Africa some years earlier had been accompanied by considerable publicity and mass meetings throughout the country. But in 1958 it was Britain, rather than South Africa, which was the context for racial violence, as the streets of Notting Hill and Nottingham exploded during the August bank-holiday period. The violence, which involved mainly white youths from districts such as Notting Hill and Shepherd's Bush which were mainly or wholly white, was directed at the small West Indian community. As Ruth Glass's formative study *Newcomers: The West Indians in London* (London, 1960) was later to show, a climate of violence had been built up in the area by the activities of various 'Keep Britain White' groups. Huddleston himself was living in Notting Hill, where he was prior of the Mirfield house in Holland Park. I was in the East End, living in Cable Street, at that time the social centre of the London Docks and the heart of what was misleadingly termed 'the coloured quarter'. It was there that we first met.

No. 84 Cable Street had been a brothel until, in 1944, Father Neville Palmer and Father Charles Preston, members of the Society of St Francis, converted it into St Francis' Hospice. From then until the early 1960s it remained as a house of hospitality within the Cable Street community. Neville had been a novice with Trevor Huddleston at Mirfield many years before, and in 1959 he invited him to stay in Cable Street and preach to the small, mainly black congregation which met there on Sunday mornings. Trevor was due to arrive for what Neville somewhat euphemistically described as 'dinner' at 7 p.m. By two minutes past he had not arrived, so Neville announced that he was going visiting. When the distinguished visitor arrived, we were to deliver him to the home of one of the local families. At that point, however, Trevor appeared, carrying a large suitcase. 'Oh, yes, very good to see you', murmured Neville in his usual matter-of-fact way. 'Put that case down there. We're just going to visit some local families.' And off they went—with no sign of dinner. At about 9.30 p.m. they both reappeared. Neville said to me, 'Ken, please ask Brother Gordon to prepare the dinner. It's a boiled egg.' I always associated Trevor Huddleston with boiled eggs from that day onwards.

It was symbolic that his first public visit to the East End should have been to Cable Street. For it was here that, during the 1940s, the first sizeable black community had grown up in the East End. It was the sociologist Michael Banton who, in a study published in 1955 and based on his doctoral thesis, termed it 'the coloured quarter', though the actual ratio of Afro-Caribbean and Asian people in the neighbourhood was very small. Nor was Cable Street itself a mainly black street: the vast majority of the population were white, and east of Cannon Street Road one rarely saw a black face. But when people spoke of Cable Street it was the western end that they usually had in mind. Here was about a half mile of cafés and clubs: Howard's (Nigerian) Café with the Tequila Club beneath it, Hassan's Rio Club for the Somalis, Bruno's and Valetta Maltese cafés, the Yugoslavia Café, the Rainbow (Gambian) Café, and many others catering for people from East, West, and North Africa, Malta, and various parts of Asia. The original Arab café in the East End was just round the corner in Leman Street, adjoining the Brown Bear pub, while for a time the world headquarters of the 'Liberal Party of Malta', led by one Carmelo Gauci, was at 82 Cable Street. Its window had 'icons' of Our Lady, the Sacred Heart, and Joe Grimond, before which coloured votive lights burned!

The café quarter had come into existence towards the end of

the 1940s. In 1947 there were accounts in the local press of gang warfare between West Africans and other groups, and in the same year over 3,000 people signed a petition to Stepney Council about conditions in the cafés and pubs. The last few months of 1947 saw a series of wildly exaggerated articles about the black community in what the popular Press were now calling 'London's Harlem'. Thus Vivien Batchelor wrote in *John Bull*: 'Seamen all over the world know of Cable Street, and if their tastes lie that way, make for it as soon as their ships dock. Some of them are coloured boys just off their first ship. A few months ago they were still half naked in the bush.' The story (which survived into the 1960s) that policemen only walked in pairs in Cable Street dates from this period, though *Reynolds News* printed a photograph of a solitary policeman in Cable Street at night, while its disappointed reporter commented: 'In the hours I spent in the Cable Street area, I saw no fight, heard no quarrel, did not even see a drunken person.'

One of the few balanced accounts from these early years was a talk by Patrick O'Donovan on 'The Challenge of Cable Street' given on BBC radio in February 1950. O'Donovan rightly pointed out that the street was 'not extraordinary except maybe for the first hundred yards' and that 'the majority of the street deeply resent the name it has been given'. Yet he reported that, within the first few hundred yards, there was 'a sense of hopelessness and a poverty that has ceased to struggle. It is as bad as anything I have ever seen in London. . . . I think these few hundred yards are about the most terrible in London.'

The sadness and despair was a feature of the neighbourhood which was noted by many writers. A black American, Roi Ottley, wrote a highly dramatic and not very accurate account in his book *No Green Pastures* (London, 1952). Cable Street was described here as 'a dismal negro slum'. Ottley went on: 'Few slums in the United States compare with this area's desperate character, unique racial composition, and atmosphere of crime, filth and decay.' He contrasted the life of the cafés and clubs in Cable Street with the 'good natured exuberance' of taverns in Harlem. By contrast, the atmosphere in Cable Street was 'mysterious, sinister and heavily laden with surreptitious violence'. The contrast or comparison with Harlem was a frequent one in the media, and when I lived in Cable Street there was one café called Little Harlem Café which had made use of this part of the mythology.

Cable Street was a very violent street but little of the violence was interracial. Most of the fights were typical dockland quarrels between seamen and prostitutes. The organized prostitution in the East End centred on Cable Street, Commercial Road, and the adjacent side-streets, and most of the prostitutes were young girls from Ireland, Scotland, and the North of England. The British Social Biology Council's study of prostitution in 1955 used the term 'Stepney problem' to describe the situation in Cable Street. 'Mentally, morally and physically, they were in a lower grade than the ordinary prostitute', the study concluded.

There was also the violence associated with the appalling housing and the stress it caused within families. But of racially motivated violence one saw little. A well-known figure in the seamen's union, George Foulser, one of the relatively small number of white men who spent a good deal of time in the cafés, wrote a somewhat romanticized article in the *Observer* in 1960 entitled 'Cablestrasse', in which he rejected the conventional view of the street, preferring to portray it in a more cheerful and friendly way. 'It is a place with an atmosphere of its own, a combination of British and overseas traditions. From all over the world, people have travelled to settle in Cablestrasse; to live and work together as peaceful fellow-citizens. They are an object lesson in living for other people everywhere.' In contrast to Foulser's account, Ashley Smith in his book *The East Enders* (London, 1961) described it as 'the filthiest, dirtiest, most repellently odoured street in Christendom'.

However, while there was not much evidence of racial violence in 1958, there were two reasons why some of the population felt they had good cause to worry. One was that the Notting Hill disturbances had involved a small black community in areas which were mainly white, although that community was more dispersed than the black population of Cable Street. There was a fear that the pattern of invading gangs of youths coming into districts with minorities of black people might spread from the west to the east. There was some movement between the two areas. Colin MacInnes, whose novel *Absolute Beginners* is set within the context of the Notting Hill riots, was often in Cable Street and was a well-known face around the African cafés. He was one of the links between the Notting Hill and East End communities, and my memory is that he was one of the people who expressed fears that the violence might spread. Linked with this was the fact that the immediate reaction to the violence in Notting Hill, particularly from some Labour MPs, was a demand for control of black immigration. Black people had no reason to look for support to the Labour Party, which had showed little interest in their presence and which, in both the East End and Notting Hill, was riddled with racism. And so the black community in Cable Street had good cause to fear that the violence and the anti-black campaign would not stop at Ladbroke Grove.

The second reason for fear was due to historical and geographical features in the East End itself. Anti-Jewish feelings had been stirred up in the early 1900s by such figures as Arnold White and Major Evans Gordon, the MP for Stepney and one of the founders of the British Brothers' League. In the 1930s Mosley's British Union of Fascists had been strong in the Shoreditch, Bethnal Green, and Limehouse areas. In 1936 Cable Street itself had been the scene of the famous battle—though it was the police, not the Fascists, who got hurt there. The Battle of Cable Street did not bring an end to the Fascist presence in the East End, and Mosley's activity increased for a time after October 1936. After the war Mosley returned to East London, concentrating more on Dalston, but standing for Shoreditch and Finsbury as a parliamentary candidate in 1965. In the early 1960s there were rumours that the Union Movement were trying to exploit the Cable Street situation.

However, it was other small Fascist and racist groups which paid most attention to the Cable Street area. On 29 May 1958 an East London branch of the National Labour Party (NLP) was formed at the Carpenters' Arms in Cheshire Street, Bethnal Green. At this meeting it was agreed that an intensive anti-immigrant propaganda campaign would be launched in the area. In 1960 swastikas appeared on the wall of Stepney

Green Synagogue. In the same year the NLP merged with Colin Jordan's White Defence League (which had been active in Notting Hill) to form the British National Party (BNP). The BNP newspaper *Combat* took a considerable interest in the black community in Cable Street. During the early part of 1961 the BNP was holding regular meetings at the corner of Cheshire Street and Kerbela Street, an old-established Fascist 'pitch'. *Combat* was announcing 'Stepney vice is a black problem'. Stepney, it claimed, was 'a stinking cess-pit that is a mecca for every black pimp and dope addict who steps off the immigrant boat and for every white slut who can hitch her way to London from all corners of Britain'. It went on to speak of the previous five years: 'In those five years, from Stepney's MP, Mr W. J. Edwards, and from the LCC, has come nothing! It has been left to the British National Party speakers at their regular Sunday meeting pitch in nearby Bethnal Green to denounce this blot on the face of East London.' The Bethnal Green area had been safe Fascist territory since the 1930s. Even further back, Jewish children at the turn of the century would be warned by their parents against walking through Bethnal Green at night. The district around the northern part of Brick Lane and Bethnal Green Road was again to figure in the story of East End Fascism in the peak period of National Front activity in the late 1970s.

Fascism always builds upon existing discontents and inequalities and translates them into prejudice and hatred. And undoubtedly there was enough raw material and to spare in Cable Street. Here were conditions which, in the memorable words of Father Joseph Williamson, parish priest of St Paul's, Dock Street, in the 1950s and early 1960s, were 'worse than those for pigs on a modern farm'. (When he first uttered those words about a particular property, the landlord threatened libel proceedings until he discovered that Williamson planned to defend himself and to turn the court into a campaigning ground for his anti-slums crusade. He then swiftly lowered the rents and improved the property!) Many of those who suffered the worst conditions in the area were black immigrants. The immigrants in Cable Street fell into two main categories: those (mainly West African and Somali) who had come originally as seamen and had settled in the area; and those more recent immigrants from the Caribbean who had come as a response to unemployment at home and the recruiting campaign launched by the British government. These immigrants were desperately needed on the labour market but little provision was made for them on the housing market. It was their labour that was wanted, not their presence. They had not created the conditions in Cable Street, which was notorious in the nineteenth century. But they were blamed for them.

The saga of Cable Street housing is one of the most depressing episodes in recent East End history. It is of crucial importance in understanding the shape that British racism has taken. Here a black community was 'ghettoized', criminalized, and isolated from access to the centres of power. Cable Street was seen as somehow separate from the rest of the East End. The London County Council was embarrassed by Cable Street and avoided acting against the conditions until the publicity made continued delay impossible. The ruling Labour group on Stepney Council pretended that the blacks were not there. Certainly they were not in the Labour Party. Only the three Communists—Solly Kaye, Barney Borman, and Max Levitas—and the Independent (ex-Labour, later Liberal) Edith Ramsey took any notice of what was going on. Solly Kaye was a legendary figure in the East End. Years after he had left the district, a piece of graffiti proclaiming 'Vote for Solly Kaye' remained on a wall on the newly built Granby Street Estate in Bethnal Green. Kaye was a charismatic orator, and his election meetings resembled old-fashioned revival meetings (though without any reference to God!) He was once described by a local priest as the one surviving prophet of the Lord amid all the prophets of Baal in Stepney Council.

But the key figure in the campaign against the slum conditions was undoubtedly Father Joe Williamson. Throughout most of his time in Stepney, he worked in close collaboration with Edith Ramsey, the formidable Principal of Stepney Evening Institute. Had it not been for Ramsey and Williamson, it is likely that the conditions in Cable Street would have deteriorated even further. Both of them were highly effective campaigners, publicists, and articulate protagonists of their cause. Yet neither of them was capable of mobilising in a political way.

Both were highly individualistic and idiosyncratic in their style of operation. Ramsey was a maverick who was terrified of Communism and feared that black people might be led in a leftist direction. As early as 1950 she was warning that Communists were infiltrating the Somali community. One of her main arguments for better social provision for immigrants was that it would make Communist activity less likely and Communism less attractive. Her private papers, now housed in the local-history room at Mile End Library, bring this anti-Communist element out very clearly. Her knowledge of the East End and its history, as well as of its subcultures and byways, particularly the world of prostitution, was encyclopaedic. Her devotion to people in need, particularly in housing need, made her one of the most beloved figures in Stepney. The Somalis were particularly devoted to her for her pioneering work in the teaching of English through her evening classes. She was an old-fashioned 'maternalist' do-gooder in the best East End tradition.

Williamson was a devout eccentric and acted on impulse and with great fervour. His strength lay in his naïvety and his unpredictability. Nobody knew what he would do next. There was a flavour of Saul Alinsky about him, though I am sure he had never heard of Alinsky and he lacked Alinsky's political skill. But Alinsky's three maxims—never tell the enemy what you're going to do, never do the same thing twice, and always act with humour—might have been used as a summary of Williamson's approach. His pamphlets and parish magazines (all of which were propaganda for his cause) were always sent to the Royal Family and the whole of the media. He knew how to use them for his own ends, and for the purposes of what he always referred to as 'The Work'. Williamson achieved what many more careful and more rational people would never have achieved. On one occasion the LCC held its first all-night sitting for over twenty years as a result of a published claim by Williamson that they had become landlords to 'a vast and shameful brothel' in Stepney. He constantly bombarded all authorities from the Prime Minister downwards with his campaign material, with detailed photographs of the conditions he described. When the demolition of Sander Street—the street which had been at the centre of the LCC controversy—

began at seven one morning, Williamson was there, kneeling in the street reciting the Gloria—and the *Daily Mail* just happened to be passing by at the time and were able to photograph him. (In fact, his friend and churchwarden Frank Rust was a *Mail* photographer, and there was a very effective partnership between them.)

Williamson did not suffer fools gladly, and was scathing in his denunciations of those who were less than whole-hearted in their support of 'The Work'. He had nothing but contempt—which he had no hesitation in expressing publicly —for Stepney's MP Walter Edwards, and had no qualms about inviting other MPs into the area in the hope that they might act where the local member had, in his view, dismally failed to do so. On the other hand, in spite of his own fierce anti-Communism, he was very favourably disposed towards Solly Kaye, whom he saw as an ally in the battle against slum landlords. His relations with his fellow clergy were ambivalent. He was inclined to assume that those who did not publicly speak out on slums and prostitution were apathetic or were not on his side.

Williamson's naïvety was at the heart of his success, but it also had grave dangers. Because he was so individualistic, he was never able to work with an organized movement; and his support for immigration control was used by racist and Fascist groups for their own purposes. The BNP praised him as 'one of the few churchmen who have the courage to speak out against the vice problems brought in by immigrants'. Some of the people to whom Williamson turned for help in promoting 'The Work' used language which was hardly designed to promote good race relations in Stepney, or to improve Williamson's own credibility in the eyes of the black community. One such was the journalist Beverley Nichols, whose article in the *Sunday Dispatch* in 1961 was reprinted and circulated by Williamson in support of his work. Nichols described the problem of Cable Street as 'a black problem . . . Through all the squalid tangle of this dustbin area stalks the figure of the coloured man.' He wrote of 'the tens of thousands of coloured men from all over the Commonwealth who have flocked to the shelter of the Welfare State'. Williamson accepted support fairly uncritically. Unlike his predecessor

John Groser, he seemed to do nothing to protect himself against being used by elements in the mass media and others with motives and positions very different from his own. With his simple and single vision, he probably believed that it was he who was making use of them in the service of his campaigns. He never saw the wider implications of his words and actions. In his political innocence, he assumed that those good Tory MPs who descended on Stepney and denounced its Labour Council and the Labour LCC, not to mention its Labour MP, were all motivated by nothing but goodwill and concern for the people of the neighbourhood.

For the most part, the churches of the East End, like the Council, ignored Cable Street. The rector of the parish which included most of the 'coloured quarter' was rarely seen in the street. During the time that I lived in the street, I had no sense that the clergy or members of the churches showed any sign of wanting to get to know the black community or to find out anything about them: where they came from, what they thought, what their experience was. As far as the Church of England was concerned, the particular form that Anglicanism took in Stepney probably did not help the churches to relate to the black community or to the issues of racial oppression. Most of Stepney, like Notting Hill, was Anglo-Catholic in its tradition. In spite of radical figures like John Groser, the Anglo-Catholic subculture did not possess the resources to help it grapple with changing social reality. Many of these churches had become citadels of illusion, pockets of escape from the real world into a grotto of pietism, places of refuge for those threatened by social change. They represented a backward-looking force and, in relation to the black community, a racist force.

Of course, that is not the whole story. There were individual clergy—John Groser, Jack Boggis, the Franciscans, among others—who, from the earliest days of immigration, were active in care for the new community and in resistance to racism. Later, when immigration from the Caribbean increased, churches of Anglo-Catholic tradition, particularly in Hackney, played an important pastoral role. But in Stepney my impression was that Anglo-Catholicism was, by the 1950s and 1960s, a reactionary force, and those most closely identified with that tradition showed no sign of real concern with the growth of racism.

By the early 1960s Cable Street was dying. The agitation about the slum conditions had gone on for over twenty years. A group of local clergy in 1947 had called for 'special priority' to be given to Cable Street. But it was not until 1967 that any major clearance work took place. 'Everything happens in Cable Street', commented Sarah in Arnold Wesker's *Chicken Soup with Barley*. The 1960s experience was that things were always on the point of happening. The Minister of Housing, Henry Brooke, in a letter to Father Williamson on 16 August 1960, claimed that redevelopment had been speeded up 'after a meeting of Ministers at the Home Office in 1958'! A report to the LCC Town Planning Sub-committee in 1961 described the property as 'in a declining state', and stressed 'the need to speed up redevelopment'. In May 1961 the Housing Committee Chairman Norman Pritchard claimed that 'some large-scale demolition has started'. However, it was difficult for the residents of the street to identify where exactly this was taking place. In July 1962 Brooke's successor, Sir Keith Joseph, responding during a Commons debate to one of Williamson's pamphlets, opposed any pause in slum clearance on the grounds that 'it is Cable Street that we would be pausing at'. In July 1964 yet another report from the Town Planning Sub-committee noted, with some understatement, that the area had been 'the subject of considerable publicity during 1961–2'. These LCC reports led to a spate of optimistic predictions in the Press, and this was probably their purpose. 'Death sentence for Cable Street E.1. and they all rejoice', ran one headline. 'The End of Vice Mile' was another. The LCC repeated, 'We want to see this area cleared up very soon.' However, Lena Jeger, writing in the *Guardian* in 1963, was more realistic. Cable Street, she said, was 'as unlucky as it is notorious'. In fact, as late as January 1967, the main structure of the 'coloured quarter' remained exactly as it always had been.

Meanwhile, Brick Lane and Old Montague Street were taking over as centres of the Asian community in the East End. The cafés were moving and so were the prostitutes. A new community, mainly from East Pakistan, was moving into the area. Brick Lane had been the heart of the Jewish ghetto at the turn of the century. Now it was becoming the home for a new community.

Nationally too the scene was changing between 1961 and 1967. The Commonwealth Immigrants Act of 1962 had brought an end to primary immigration from the 'New Commonwealth'. The Labour Party, which, under Gaitskell, had opposed the legislation, had, in 1965, renewed and strengthened it. The White Paper of that year went a long way towards meeting the demands of the 'Keep Britain White' groups. By 1965 black people were seen as intrinsically undesirable. Racial discrimination at the doors of Britain was seen as the necessary condition of good race relations inside Britain. The path for the creation of cruder racist groups was prepared. In 1966 the National Front was created from a merger of the League of Empire Loyalists and the British National Party, to be joined in 1967 by the more explicitly Nazi Greater Britain Movement. But its progress was very slow. On 20 April 1968, Enoch Powell delivered his infamous 'rivers of blood' speech at Birmingham. By focusing on the issues of race and immigration, Powell probably helped to undermine the potential growth in support for the National Front for some years. Its day was to come after 1972. Of course, in a sense the Front was irrelevant. For racism was no longer the preserve of small 'extreme' groups. It had been incorporated into the state plan. Racism had been nationalized. Positions which would have horrified Gaitskell and the more liberal Tories of the early 1960s were now accepted as the basis of policy. The genteel racism of the major parties was now a far more serious issue than the National Front and its satellites. Nevertheless at the local level the Front was to play a critical role in the organization of racial hatred.

Perhaps the first sign that organized racial hatred was returning to the East End was the emergence in 1969 of 'Paki-bashing'. There had been some earlier attacks on Pakistani men in the Euston area in 1967. But it was in 1969–70 that 'Paki-bashing' became identified as part of the way of life of some sections of youth culture. The term itself originated in the East End, probably on the Collingwood Estate in Bethnal

Green. Historically it was associated with the emergence of the 'skinhead' culture among working-class white kids, though it is wrong to assume that all skinheads were racists. How the organized racist groups related to the violence is not clear. Some would claim that they orchestrated it, and this is certainly true in part of the late period. It is more likely that they, along with developments within the national scene, created a climate in which racial violence and bigotry were more acceptable and respectable.

The racial violence was directed almost entirely against the growing community from East Pakistan. The period between March and May 1970 was the crucial period for the escalation of violence. The first Press reference seems to have been on 3 April when several papers reported attacks on two Asian workers at the Chest Hospital in Bethnal Green. On 5 April the *Observer* gave the phenomenon its first public identification. 'The name of the game is Paki-bashing. In London's East End, the skinheads might have learned the rules from the Hitler youth. Any Asian careless enough to be walking the streets alone at night is a fool.' On 26 April fifty skinheads rampaged through Brick Lane attacking both people and property within the Pakistani area. Nevertheless the police were reluctant to attribute racial motives for the attacks. A senior CID officer was quoted on 13 April as saying, 'I don't believe there are gangs which are deliberately going out with the intention of beating up Pakistanis.'

Although there had been a small community from Bengal in the East End since the 1940s, the growth of the new community around Brick Lane occurred after 1960. Almost without exception the immigrants were from the rural area of Sylhet. There were three phases of the immigration: the phase of male migrant workers between 1960 and 1970; the early 1970s phase, the period of the struggle for independence and the creation of Bangladesh, when more families came; and the period following Bangladesh independence when large numbers of dependants arrived. The geographic concentration of the community was already clear in its main outlines by the 1961 Census. Brick Lane, the former Jewish social centre, now became the heart of the Asian community of Spitalfields.

Brick Lane had a somewhat different history from Cable

Street. It was older, being one of the first parts of the East End
to be built up. Its origins go back to 1576 when a Roman
cemetery at Lolesworth Field was broken up for brick
manufacture, and it was this which gave the street its name.
Whereas in 1670 it was described as a 'deep dirty road', by
1748 a writer called it 'a well paved street'. Both Brick Lane
and the side-streets running off it were completely built up by
the middle of the eighteenth century. In the mid-nineteenth
century there were, according to Mayhew, a considerable
number of brothels and lodging-houses in these streets, and it
was here later in that century that Jack the Ripper committed
his murders. Brick Lane was, according to the Rector of
Christ Church, Spitalfields, in the 1880s, 'a land of beer and
blood'. But within a decade the lane had been transformed by
the settlement of East European Jews, and between 1880 and
1905 Brick Lane became the main street of the East End
Jewish ghetto. But the northern part of it, in Bethnal Green,
remained solidly English, and it was here that anti-Semitism
and later Fascism took root. As early as 1892 candidates in the
South West Bethnal Green ward (the northern part of Brick
Lane) were campaigning on an anti-aliens ticket. The role of
Bethnal Green as the base for organized racism had been
established. In the 1930s Sir Oswald Mosley was to build on
this tradition, and Bethnal Green and Shoreditch were the key
districts for the organized Fascist campaign.

So when in 1965 Sir Oswald Mosley made his last attempt
to re-enter Parliament as candidate for Shoreditch and
Finsbury, he was on very familiar territory. A year later the
National Front was formed, and the area around Hyde Road
and Whitmore Road in Shoreditch was to become one of its
strongholds. It was, however, not until the mid-1970s that the
NF was to become a significant and frightening presence in
the East End. At the General Election in October 1974, the
NF gained 9.4 per cent of the poll in Hackney South and
Shoreditch (the highest in Britain) and 7.6 per cent in Bethnal
Green and Bow (the fifth highest in Britain.) By the time of
the GLC elections in 1977 they gained 19 per cent in Hackney
South and Shoreditch. This period also saw the spread of NF
slogans and racist graffiti all over the Bethnal Green area.
There is little if any evidence of people being charged for

painting racist graffiti, but in August 1977 five trade-unionists were arrested for removing some graffiti from a railway bridge. When the case eventually came to court in December, it was dismissed. But the fact that the case could have been brought at all reinforced the widespread belief in the East End that the police regarded anti-racists with greater hostility than racists.

The mid-1970s also saw the escalation of racial violence, not only in the East End but elsewhere. The magazine *Race Today* in June 1976 listed thirty cases of racial attacks which had taken place in the East End between March and May of that year. Fuller documentation was presented in a report *Blood on the Streets*, published by Bethnal Green and Stepney Trades Council in 1978. During this period, the NF were active every Sunday at the corner of Brick Lane and Bethnal Green Road, and many observers saw a connection between the inflammatory material which was being distributed there and the violence which was taking place in nearby streets. In May 1977 *Race Today* called for self-defence patrols in the district in the face of 'a systematic campaign of deadly assaults against the Asian community'. In October 1977 around 5,000 people marched through the NF strongholds in Shoreditch and Bethnal Green to a multiracial rock festival in Victoria Park. In December the dismissal of the case against the removers of racist graffiti gave others confidence to follow their example, and an entire wall of NF slogans, swastikas, and assorted Fascist and racist graffiti on the Cheshire Street baths was cleaned up. Even a British Movement badge which had adorned the outside wall of Bethnal Green police station for months was finally removed. But as the year ended *The Times* dismally reported, 'Police initiative fails to halt wave of violence against Asians.

It was 1978 which was the critical year both for racial violence and for the mobilization of anti-racists against the NF presence in the area. The highly successful rock festival of October 1977 was followed in May by a much bigger, nationally organized Carnival Against the Nazis, on May Day 1978. Over 80,000 people marched, with bands and banners, from Trafalgar Square to Victoria Park. It was a remarkable event and gave a tremendous boost of morale to those who were organizing against the NF in the East End. But a few days later, on 4 May, there occurred an event which was to change the course of the anti-racist struggle. On that day, in Adler Street, close to Brick Lane, a young Bengali clothing worker, Altab Ali, was murdered. The murder sparked off a series of demonstrations and led to the increased mobilization of the Bangladeshi community in the struggle against racism. On 14 May about 7,000 Bengalis marched to Downing Street behind Altab Ali's coffin. The march was one of the biggest and most impressive demonstrations of Asian solidarity ever held in Britain. Very old men marched beside representatives of the newly radicalized Bengali youth.

A month later two incidents occurred almost simultaneously which together marked a major turning-point in the Bengali response. The first was the proposal by the Greater London Council to set aside certain blocks of flats exclusively for Bengali people. The second was the mass invasion of Brick Lane by several hundred skinheads. The origins of the GLC proposal, which became known as the 'ghetto plan', go back to a report on *Housing of Bengalis in the London Borough of Tower Hamlets*, presented on 22 May 1978 by the GLC's Director of Housing, Leonard Bennett. In this report Bennett suggested that the GLC might meet the wishes of the Bengali community to be housed in safe areas 'by earmarking blocks of flats, or indeed a whole estate if necessary, for their community'. He concluded with a formal request to the Council that he should be authorized 'to set aside a few blocks of flats in or near Spitalfields specifically for the occupation of people from Bangladesh'. There was no use of the word 'ghetto', but on 4 June the *Observer* ran an article headed 'GLC Plans Ghetto for Bengalis'. The following week saw a whole series of articles in the media on the ghetto theme. On 6 June, the *Daily Telegraph*, in a typically unpleasant editorial, made an observation which was to prove painfully prophetic. After pointing out that ghettos were 'not an obviously bad thing', the editorial went on to say that their creation should not be discouraged since 'there will be fewer cases of friction if races live separately. Admittedly there will be forays into those areas by hooligans of other races. But, alas, the harmonious, multi-racial Utopia cannot exist outside the minds of those who are striving so disastrously to bring it about.' Five days later, on Sunday, 11 June, a foray of hooligans into Brick Lane did in fact take place. Several hundred youths rampaged through the district, smashing windows, throwing bottles and lumps of concrete, and damaging shops and cars.

It was the mass violence of 11 June which led to renewed concern with the NF activity in Bethnal Green Road and Brick Lane. For some two years the NF, along with other racist and Fascist groups, had maintained a regular presence in the area, and their presence had coincided with the deterioration of race relations and the increase of violence. The police view was that the NF were not contravening any laws, and policemen in private were often heard to express the view that the anti-racists who drew attention to and opposed the Fascist presence were more troublesome than the NF themselves were. Towards the end of June, at a meeting in the Montefiore Centre, Superintendent John Wallis, a respected police officer responsible for community relations work, made the (from his perspective) unfortunate statement that the police were impartial in the protection they gave to the NF, and went on to suggest that anti-racists who objected to the NF should turn up first! A few days later, in a letter which was published in the two East End newspapers, I thanked John Wallis for his support, and called upon all anti-racists to implement his suggestion.

The following months saw a growing opposition to the Fascist presence. Beginning with a relatively small number of people, mainly associated with Tower Hamlets Movement Against Racism and Fascism (THMARF), occupying the NF pitch from about 6 a.m. on Sunday morning, the numbers grew quickly into thousands. Within a short time, the police decided that a breach of the peace was likely to occur if anti-racists continued to occupy the site which the NF (who were now nowhere to be seen) had occupied for several years, and the site was sealed off by a massive police presence. But anti-racists from all over Greater London and other parts of the country continued to gather every Sunday in the Brick Lane area. The words 'Brick Lane' had become a symbol of the struggle against organized racism. More than once during these months I met determined-looking young people in

Bethnal Green, wearing badges saying 'Brick Lane Against the Nazis', who stopped me and asked, 'Could you tell me the way to Brick Lane?' On the other hand, the local Bengali community became increasingly involved in the street activity. The NF were forced out of the area, and, although they later returned on a smaller scale, their mass base was undermined. They had reached the peak of their success in the East End, and from then onwards their history was one of fragmentation and decline.

The 'ghetto controversy' also had continuing spin-offs. The reaction of most of the Bengali groups to the Bennett proposal was hostile. The mainly white tenants' groups were outraged. Ironically it was this proposal which brought together, and helped to forge new unities between, groups of white residents and Bengali organizations. On 6 June a meeting was called by Spitalfields Friends and Neighbours and the Chicksand Community Action Group, and they were joined by representatives of the Spitalfields Bengali Action Group, the Bangladesh Youth Movement, and the Bangladesh Youth Association. All those present opposed any suggestion of a 'ghetto'. A letter sent by the five groups condemned the plan which, they claimed, 'would play into the hands of those who preach and use violence'. Throughout the controversy it would seem that the only support for the idea came from the *Daily Telegraph* and the National Front. Martin Webster, at that time one of the NF leaders, said that a ghetto was 'the best thing to do until such people can be humanely repatriated'. The Bengali Housing Action Group (BHAG), the only group named in Bennett's document as a source for his idea, denied that such a plan was their intention. What they had urged was that Bengalis should be rehoused on safe estates where they would be free from racial violence, and they had identified thirteen such estates. In their statement *Asians and Housing: The Bengali Housing Action Group Statement*, issued in June 1978, they referred to the GLC proposal.

At no stage did we ask for a 'ghetto'. Nor did we ask for segregated slum blocks to be set aside for our members. If this is what the GLC propose, we intend to fight them in the same way that we have fought them before. We will not settle for segregated slums.

And in this response they spoke for the entire Bengali community.

The police role throughout the entire period of escalating racial violence and the growing Fascist activity was at best unhelpful, and at worst contributed to the climate of tension and suspicion. Police officers were reluctant to accept the reality of racial attacks, and it took about fifteen years and numerous reports, including one from the Home Office itself, to convince them that racial attacks were common and increasing. The lack of confidence in the police among the Bengali community was due to a combination of factors: the refusal to take their complaints seriously, the repeated cases of long delays in responding to calls for help, and the lack of action on the intimidating Fascist presence in the area. Many Bengalis reported that when they rang the police to report a violent incident, the only result was that, when the police eventually arrived, they questioned the callers themselves about their immigration status. But there was another factor which was stressed in a report by two local youth workers, Caroline Adams and John Newbiggin:

In Bengali eyes young white men with short hair and big boots are in the National Front until proved otherwise. Not only do the police fit the physical description, but they are drawn from the same age groups, the same class, the same estates, the same pubs, as the NF.

Moreover, the open expression of sympathy for the NF by police officers in Bethnal Green was by no means unusual. The opponents of the NF were seen as the real troublemakers. In fact, it was only when anti-racists took action against the NF presence that the police took any action—though usually against the anti-racists. It was only after the incidence of racial attacks had been demonstrated beyond all reasonable doubt that the police themselves drew attention to the issue and expressed their concern. But it was fifteen years too late. As far as the Bengali community were concerned, the police could not be relied upon to oppose racism in the same way as they might be relied on, for example, to oppose attacks on property. Even there, attacks on Bengali property seemed to have lower priority.

The white Left, who were active in THMARF and in the

Anti-Nazi League (ANL), were a small and weak minority in relation to the population of the East End. The Communist Party, which at one time had been solidly Jewish and very well organized in Stepney, was now a much-diminished group. The Socialist Workers' Party, who were the motive force behind the ANL and Rock Against Racism, tended to see themselves as an enlightened vanguard who had 'learnt the lessons of history', and could inject that knowledge into the mass of the people. In practice, they concentrated very much on street confrontations, giving the impression to the local community that they were simply a mirror image of the NF. Their literature was smug and arrogant: only they knew the answer to Fascism, and they hoped that the Bengalis would catch up one day. At the local level, the Socialist Unity/International Marxist Group (IMG) members were more sensitive to the need for a wider campaign which attended to the feelings and the unheard voices of local people, and which moved beyond the immediate Fascist presence to the underlying causes of support for the Fascist movement. The Labour Party, with the exception of a small group of dedicated activists, was unreliable and ambivalent on racism. Some of the right-wing Labour councillors would privately express views which were not far removed from those of the NF (who drew most of their East End support from disillusioned Labour voters). I recall one occasion before the GLC elections, when a group of us in THMARF called a meeting of local political groups to discuss a common statement on racism and Fascism. The people in the room quickly divided. On one side, the Conservatives and the Communists wanted a general statement which all could sign, a vague 'We oppose racism' kind of statement, which avoided potentially divisive areas such as the NF, racial attacks, housing allocations, and immigration control procedures. On the other were the IMG, the Socialist Feminists, and the church representatives calling for a concrete commitment to certain positions. In the middle was the Labour Party, in effect saying, 'We don't mind what you say, but if the Tories sign it, we won't.'

This is not to deny that there were not some very significant gains from within the Left groups. They all took organized racism far more seriously than did the major parties. Without individuals such as Chris Searle, Claire Weingarten, Belle Harris, and Dan Jones (the last two being Labour Party members), among others, the opposition to the NF would never have grown to a well-organized force. Some of the small Left groups organized protection for Asian families on dangerous estates, and while they were criticized for 'making political capital' out of people's sufferings, their critics, for the most part, made no effort to provide equivalent levels of support.

But the real contribution of the white Left groups lay more at a theoretical and long-term level. The struggle to have the issues of racism and the oppression of blacks, as well as those of the oppression of women and of sexual minorities, accepted as essential elements of a socialist agenda, was fought originally within the Trotskyist Left. That struggle was a twofold one: to prevent these issues being lost by being absorbed within 'the class struggle' in a way which ignored the specificity and distinct character of these forms of oppression, and, on the other hand, to resist a politics which concerned itself with the 'new social movements' in a way which ignored class politics altogether. It was a struggle to make and maintain connections. Although they were small, these groups contained some of the key thinkers who were to help to change and widen the horizons of socialist thought in the 1980s. The impact of the anti-racist struggles of the late 1970s is still being felt within the socialist movement, and the areas which it opened up will not go away, however uncomfortable they may be for the Labour leadership.

But it was the growing involvement of the Bengali community which at the end of the day was the decisive feature of the East End struggle. The image of the helpless Asian victim, the passive recipient of racial aggression, was firmly rejected as a new Bengali radicalism emerged from the—almost literal—ashes of the Brick Lane conflicts. The formation in 1976 of the Anti-racist Committee of Asians in East London (ARCAEL) marked a major turning-point in Bengali attitudes and a decisive stage in the politicization of the new Bengali leadership. The activity around ARCAEL changed the consciousness of many young Bengalis and laid the foundations

for the future organized movements within the community.
Caroline Adams, the first East End youth worker to concentrate mainly on work with Bengalis, later reflected on the
ARCAEL phase. 'The Bengali community', she wrote, 'had
come of age, and could no longer be patronised or ignored, at
least not without a comeback.' The emergence of a new
Bengali radicalism was in many ways the most significant
aspect of the entire period.

How did the churches in the area respond to the threat
posed by Fascism and by racial violence? There was certainly
much concern and anxiety, and no doubt many prayers were
said. But for the most part the churches did nothing. The
clergy did not belong to the generation who had been familiar
with street protests and were, with some significant exceptions,
frightened of too close an identification with socialism. Most
of them were excellent pastors with a broadly liberal outlook
which limited their political awareness. There was fear of
contamination, and, although the NF were not exactly popular, the theology of 'leave well alone' reflected the dominant
mood. There was suspicion of conflict of any kind. Nor was
there much attempt to make contact with, let alone provide support and help for, the Bengali people. The growth
of Fascism was not seen as a matter of any great concern.
Certainly not seen as a spiritual threat. Within the churches,
life went on as usual, as if nothing had happened. On the
wider issues of state racism as manifested, for example, in the
immigration laws, the churches had little if anything to
contribute.

Together these two East End streets, Cable Street and Brick
Lane, have played a crucial role in the history of racism and
anti-racism over half a century. But their stories are very
different, as are the insights we can gain from the struggles
around them.

The Cable Street subculture of the 1940s and 1950s was
marked by a high level of despair and social fragmentation.
Ignored by the local authorities, feared by many local people,
criminalized and despised by the media, the black residents of
the street had, over the years, acquired a tragic sense of life.
There was a deep and prevailing feeling of hopelessness, a

profound and fatalist conviction that nothing would ever be done. The victim role had been accepted and internalized. In Patrick O'Donovan's words, Cable Street was characterized by 'a sense of hopelessness and a poverty that had ceased to struggle'. By contrast, the Brick Lane community fiercely rejected the victim role. Out of that 'ghetto' community came not despair but anger and organized resistance.

Again, Cable Street was marked by a general lack of interest by the black population in the politics of the area. The cultural groups were mainly tribal or national groups—the Kru Friendly Society, the Somali seamen's groups, and so on. The political concerns were those of the home countries. Brick Lane, on the other hand, experienced towards the end of the 1970s a shift from concern only with the politics of Bangladesh to a greater involvement with local issues and needs. The proliferation of youth movements, the election of Bengali councillors, the concern with issues of health care, employment, and education were all illustrative of the growing determination of the community to work for change through political organization.

The campaigns around housing, slum clearance, and the care of prostitutes in Cable Street were mainly organized by charismatic individuals who spoke (or claimed to speak) on behalf of the local people. Figures like Joe Williamson and Edith Ramsey were much loved. But they represented a kind of paternalism which was being superseded. By the time of the Brick Lane campaigns, the power and energy had shifted to communities and organized movements. The Bangladesh Youth Movement and Youth Front did not look for spokespersons outside their own ranks. A new generation of leaders was being thrown up, who had experienced racism and were determined to fight it. As far as the Church was concerned, the period between 1960 and 1980 saw a shift away from the days when the focus was on 'rescue work' and reform but with little theology, towards a more reflective and in a sense more contemplative role: of trying to share the sufferings and the aspirations of the oppressed, to seek to stand by them, not to lead but to listen, not to be figureheads but rather to be co-workers in a common project. Those church people, clergy or laity, who could not adapt to this very different style were left behind as the recognized leaders of diminishing and increasingly sectarian groups.

Some features show continuity more than contrast. In both Cable Street and Brick Lane, crude racist stereotypes of black people were built up by the media. The criminalization of the black community, the representation of black men as vicious, brutal, primitive, and dangerous, began with the media interest in Cable Street and similar districts in the 1940s and 1950s. The Brick Lane area had seen similar portrayals of the Irish and of the Jews in the nineteenth century. In recent years the language of racial polemic has become cruder and more unpleasant, and has been part of a wider culture of intolerance manifested by the popular Press against minorities of various kinds. Again, the concentration of black people in the worst housing conditions is a feature which the two streets have in common. This has led, in both cases, to the practice of treating those who suffer from housing stress or exploitation as if they were the causes of these conditions.

But the most significant change which has occurred since the early years in Cable Street has been in our understanding of racism itself. In those distant days, the word was rarely if ever used. If it was used, as by Ruth Benedict in the 1940s, it was to refer to a doctrine of racial superiority such as Nazism. In discussing actual practice, people spoke of 'the colour bar', 'the colour problem', of the need for acceptance, assimilation, integration. Black people were seen as intrinsically problematic, though regrettably necessary, additions to the labour market —a view which has continued and intensified. But racism as an integral and deeply rooted facet of white post-colonial society was not part of the conceptual framework of those days. Even in the conflict with the National Front, the tendency was to see the small racist groups as the real enemy of the British way of tolerance and liberality. Today, we see that racism is more subtle, more genteel, more centrally located within the structures and thought forms of mainstream Britain. We see that racism is more than the sum of individual feelings, prejudices, and acts of hatred, that it is a systemic reality with a life of its own. And if this is so, we must see that the struggle against racism will be hard and long.

For the vast majority of white Christian people in Britain,

the reality of racism and the potential for Fascism are not issues which are treated with any degree of theoretical or practical seriousness. On the other hand, there are signs that more Christians are recognizing the nature and dynamics of racism and Fascism, and are beginning to join forces with others in seeking to undermine these evils and create a world which more adequately reflects the demands of justice and freedom. In this shift in Christian consciousness, the influence of Trevor Huddleston, both in Africa and in East London, has been of great importance. I have argued that, in terms of the grass-roots encounter with racism and Fascism, some pointers towards a deeper understanding may also lie in study of the conflicts which occurred around these two East End streets.

Reflections from
a London Parish

FRANÇOIS PIACHAUD

IT is delightful to be invited to join in this birthday
celebration and to make a contribution to an expression of
gratitude and affection which may also serve as some record of
what a great and good man has done during the momentous
years of our time.

Others will write from positions of eminence and close
association with Bishop Huddleston's work in Africa and
England. Mine is a lesser role. I speak, as it were, from off
stage, from the point of view of a parish priest in London. I
can only describe the impact he made on many of us when he
came back from Africa a generation ago, and the inspiration
he gave us, and offer some reflections on what one learned
later through friendship.

Thirty years and more have passed, but those who were
present at those crowded public meetings in 1956 will not
forget the eloquence and moral urgency of the speaker as he
fearlessly exposed the oppression being perpetrated in South
Africa. The young priest of the Community of the Resurrection,
who had devoted his life to the people of that land, described
the indignities and sufferings of the people he loved and who
loved him, and whom he had been compelled to leave. He told
how a community like Sophiatown, which, despite poverty
and squalor, had been vibrant with vitality and friendliness,
had been crushed remorselessly at the dictate of apartheid. He
spoke of the efforts of the people to secure some measure of
freedom and justice and how violence and suppression was the

response of the white government which claimed to represent Christian civilization.

In that struggle it was 'the fierce breath of totalitarianism and tyranny which first triggered off' in him 'the determination to reveal the truth'.

The truth of the situation in South Africa had to be brought home to the conscience of the Church and nation. But it was not easy and a price had to be paid. Misunderstanding and misrepresentation had to be endured by the brave men and women, church people and others, who pleaded for the oppressed in the name of Christ and humanity. (We think of Michael Scott, Bram Fischer, Hannah Stanton, and many others).

It is difficult now to recall attitudes prevalent thirty years ago. Britain still ruled much of Africa. South Africa was still in the Commonwealth and harsh racial laws were set down to the Afrikaner mentality. A bland sense of innate superiority combined with reliance on gradual evolutionary policies regarded its problems as a temporary aberration. The Church was paternalistic, middle-class, and white-dominated. Church leaders active in the struggle against colonialism were hard to find. The very idea of involvement in social and political struggles would have been anathema to the largely complacent majority.

Today, when the evils of apartheid and the blasphemy of its pseudo-theological stance are evident for all to see, we must not forget how, for many years, not least in church circles, soft speeches decried the 'raising of controversial issues', how the moral implications of political issues were blurred, and how many were ready to cry 'peace, peace', when there could be no peace without justice and compassion.

As the unfolding tragedy of South Africa develops we must remember with pain and shame that the prophetic cry of protest was not heeded in time when something might still have been done to prevent the buttressing of apartheid with all the sanctions of law and order.

Ever since those days Bishop Huddleston has been in the forefront of the struggle against racialism. Even now, as he approaches his seventy-fifth birthday, he leads the appeal to the British government not to reject what many hold to be the

1. The Community of the Resurrection, Mirfield (High Mass)

2. Making a presentation to the boxer Jake Tuli, 1953

3. At a protest meeting, 1953

4. A farewell concert in Trevor Huddleston's honour, Johannesburg, January 1956

5. Bishop of Masasi on consecration day, Feast of St Andrew, 30 November 1960

6. Bishop of Masasi, 1962

7. Sunday Eucharist in Masasi Cathedral

8. Enthronement as Bishop of Mauritius, 1978 (Dean Paul Cathan to left of picture)

9. Trevor Huddleston's first day in Stepney, near Shadwell Basin, 1968

10. A sack-race with Chaplain Adrian Benjamin at the Arbour Youth Centre, Stepney

11. With a young friend

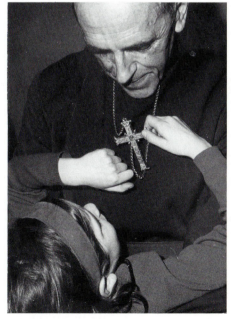

12. Trevor Huddleston receiving a standing ovation from the International Youth Conference Against Apartheid, New Delhi, 8–9 January 1987. *Left to right*: the ANC representative in India, Mr Moosa Moolla, Mr Abdul S. Minty, Honorary Secretary of the Anti-apartheid Movement and Director, World Campaign Against Military and Nuclear Collaboration with South Africa, Bishop Huddleston, Mr Anand Sharma, MP, President of the Indian Youth Congress, Prime Minister Rajiv Gandhi, and ANC Secretary General Alfred Nzo

13. At the closing session of the International Conference on Children, Repression, and the Law in Apartheid South Africa, Harare, 24–7 September 1987, convened by Trevor Huddleston. *Left to right*: Bishop Huddleston, Mr Abdul S. Minty, President Oliver Tambo, Revd Beyers Naudè, the Vice-Presidents of the Conference, and United Defence Fund representative

last means of bringing about peaceful change—especially when this rejection is based on the argument that economic sanctions would hurt the blacks, although it is they who ask for such effective measures and declare that any additional suffering that may result is preferable to the future they would otherwise face.

Of the later years and of the details of his work in Africa and England others will write from first-hand knowledge. I can only testify that, ever since 1968, when he returned from Tanzania to serve in the most depressed area of London, the name of the Bishop of Stepney has become still more widely known within and, even more, outside the Church. As the years have passed so the area and depth of his concern has grown. Through his writings, broadcasts, innumerable meetings, and travels he has reached an ever-widening audience. He stands now among the leaders in pleading the cause of the down-trodden and poor not only in Africa but in Britain and in the world. Passionately he has pleaded for Christian involvement in the struggle against the deprivation of inner cities, the appalling tide of unemployment, and the loss of dignity and hope for many thousands of young people. And he has been outspoken in criticizing the policies that, in the name of individual freedom, permit aggressive self-interest and materialism to flourish and result in a divisive society where the rich become richer and the poor poorer.

That he should stir up opposition was to be expected—and not only from those quarters that felt themselves under direct threat. The book *Naught for Your Comfort*, published in 1956 when he had to leave South Africa, soon became a best seller and is still compulsive reading. But ever since, in the circles that constitute the 'Establishment'—which might be indefinable but is not impotent—the bringer of such a discomforting message has been a marked man, to be regarded with caution and covert disapproval.

It tells us a good deal about the 'Establishment' that no place of leadership appropriate to the stature of such a man has ever been found for him in his own Church.

In fairness perhaps it should be added, since we are not depicting an archangel, such a man would not fit in comfortably with any Establishment. Apart from the fact that

to him the very idea of a Church established by act of
Parliament was (rightly) repugnant, it is evident that his
deeply personal pastoral sense was sometimes out of tune with
the multiplication of committees and paperwork that synodical
government too often seemed to involve. A certain impatience
with ecclesiastical routine and bureaucratic restraints was
what could be expected from one who did not see that his role
was to maintain the Church at ease in Zion.

Yet one cannot help but reflect sadly how different things
might have been had there been sufficient imagination and
courage to choose such a man, in his prime, to fill one of the
more important posts of leadership in the Church of England.
(Not for him, for example, would have been the response to
the crisis of religion in the post-war years that 'the revision of
the Canon Law of the Church of England is the most
absorbing and all-embracing topic'.)

Bishop Huddleston had the vision, ability, and inspiration
to be a great national leader when such leadership was sorely
needed. It is, I believe, no exaggeration to say that he held a
unique position both within the Church and outside as the
spokesman for the Christian conscience, and he had gained
the respect of many for whom ecclesiastical position meant
nothing.

Yet the Church was not prepared for bold courses. And the
reputation of a controversial figure persisted.

I have a vivid recollection of an incident many years ago when
Bishop Huddleston was first invited to address a public
meeting in one of the more affluent parishes of London on the
social and political involvement of the Church. It was in an
area where the sociological situation could be described as
cultured, urbane, and one where no parliamentary candidate
on the right wing of politics needed to feel insecure. There had
been not a few misgivings, polite, of course, but anxious,
about the advisability of inviting such a controversial speaker.
The opening minutes of the meeting were tense—and then he
had captured his audience completely. The obvious integrity
and goodness of the man shone through, and his charm. Not
all became converts to the whole message, but never again

was there a whisper of doubt. Soon he was a frequent and welcome visitor.

I mention this little incident because it was a pattern repeated again and again.

It leads to some general reflections.

In the popular mind Bishop Huddleston will always be remembered as the champion of victims of racialism and all forms of injustice. But his influence is by no means confined to his practical involvement in the immediate issues of the day. For very many he has come to represent both the moral force of a modern prophet contending for social and personal righteousness and also the spiritual and intellectual authority of a man of God who restores the credibility of the faith to contemporary doubters. I believe that it is in this dual role, distinguishable but not separable, that his significance will be assessed in history.

Let us consider the first part of this dual role. Bishop Huddleston belongs to the great socio-Catholic tradition—so largely connected with the Community of the Resurrection—where he inherited from men like Bishop Gore and Scott-Holland the concern for social justice as an inseparable part of Christian discipleship. That tradition was enhanced by William Temple and R. H. Tawney. The contribution of his own life and work is to be seen in two aspects. First he has widened the scope and area of concern for social righteousness. This he has done by confronting old problems, such as social inequality and unemployment, and also new problems, such as racial injustice and world disorder, that were hardly visible above the horizon in earlier days. Second, he has gone much further in intensifying the degree of commitment to the practical demands of social and political involvement that Christian realism requires.

In perspective it will be seen that his life and work has helped to inspire and to bring about great changes in the understanding of the role of the Church and its attitude to the world. It is premature to attempt it now but it will be a fascinating exercise for a future biographer to trace how and why the Church's apprehension of its role has changed over the last generation and to identify the part the bishop has played. It will not be easy but it will be rewarding, and it is safe to opine that it will be found that while he has been part of a developing theological-social pattern he has also been an exceptional and dynamic pioneer.

To put it in different terms we may say that he has played a leading part in the movement that may be described as the expansion of moral horizons—the realization that areas of activity formerly resigned to other governance are in fact under human control and therefore are subject to moral choice and religious insights. For example, when *laissez-faire* capitalism prevailed a Wilberforce who championed the African slave could doubt whether it would be morally right to legislate to improve the lot of his fellow-countrymen. But when the so-called iron laws of economics were seen to be neither inevitable nor immutable, but could be brought under rational control to serve the common good, it was as if a whole new field of human activity had come under moral jurisdiction and religion had to decide its attitudes to the movement for social justice. In former times the accepted philosophy had taught that the condition of the poor must be accepted as inevitable. Too often religion had been ready to declare that Providence had thus decreed it. It is the realization that such conditions are morally wrong *because* they can be altered that gives the driving force to the movement for social justice as it sweeps across the face of the earth among people of diverse religions or none.

In our own day the expansion of moral horizons reaches out to still wider areas—the unity of mankind, the building of peace, the distribution of wealth and poverty in the world—all these raise urgent moral and religious issues, and in all these matters Bishop Huddleston plays a leading part.

But there has always been reluctance on the part of some to follow the wider vision, and today there is a widespread mood of reaction. For example, it is not a little ironic that outmoded economic theories of the past are revived today, under a new name, and that it is complacently asserted that, in spite of widespread deprivation, 'There is no alternative'. And there are some who set out to undermine what the more enlightened insights of the Christian social conscience seemed to have gained. Generally they begin by emphasizing, quite rightly, that Christianity must not and cannot be identified with any particular method of social reform, and then proceed to the illegitimate conclusion that Christianity has nothing to do with social reform. In some circles there is a reaction against everything associated with 'the social gospel', and even Christian Aid is dismissed as only peripherally Christian. The bishop would be the first to admit that it is naïve to imagine that the Christian ethic can be simply transposed into a law of universal behaviour or to underestimate the depths of the human heart. Yet some of the views which are much publicized today are far more dangerously fallacious. On the one hand there is the pietistic irresponsibility of some popular evangelism that ignores the fact that redemption has to deal not only with individual sin but also with sin built into social structures, as with apartheid. On the other hand there is the pessimistic irresponsibility of 'neo-orthodoxy' that, despairing of any alleviation of the human scene, abandons the struggle for even proximate social justice and so, in effect, leaves the field to the enemy. Such attitudes are based, ultimately, on dichotomies between natural and supernatural, temporal and eternal, material and spiritual which can hold little meaning for an incarnational religion.

Against such Bishop Huddleston proclaims the gospel in its totality. It is the sovereignty of God that he sets forth by word and by life—no area of life is outside God's creative care and concern, or is irredeemable by the costly love of Christ, or is devoid of the presence of the Spirit.

We must turn now to the second aspect of Bishop Huddleston's life and work, which was described as 'helping to restore the credibility of the faith to contemporary doubters'.

Bishop Huddleston would be the first to repudiate any claim to be a theologian in the academic sense, yet many will testify to the considerable and creative part he has played in the religious scene and that his influence is by no means confined to his practical involvement in affairs.

Intellectual vigour combined with deep spirituality, integrity, and openness to fresh insights keep him sensitive to the questionings of enquiring minds. He can speak to men and women in search of a faith that can give meaning and purpose to existence and at the same time makes sense in the light of modern knowledge. Basically, his appeal derives from the recognition that truth matters supremely and that the Christian faith stands or falls by its claim to truth. He would agree that authority has a place but that it can never be a surrogate for truth. Revelation and reason cannot be in contention. Revelation is the disclosure of the living Word and all fresh knowledge of the world and man comes ultimately from God and therefore is to be welcomed. Faith involves readiness to follow wherever truth leads, in the conviction that it can never lead away from God. I believe he would endorse the view expressed in the words 'loyalty to the historic faith implies that it is the living Word which is rooted in history but is never imprisoned in the past to which we owe allegiance'.

By temperament and training belonging to the Catholic stream in the Church, he refuses to go with it when it becomes confined to narrow authoritarian channels or reacts in fearfulness of change and reform. Rather he is truly catholic in being genuinely ecumenical, and also in his outreach to other religious faiths and in his glad response to the universality of the tokens of divine presence.

It is the attitude of commitment and openness, positive and humble, that brings buoyancy and courage. There is no place in him for what was once described as an attitude of 'irreligious solicitude for the deity'. It is this kind of approach that enables him to help others to steer through the troubled waters of contemporary religious debate.

The latest theological fashion too often proves to be evanescent. For example, 'death of God theology' had no appeal for him. After a short innings, the attempt to do theology without metaphysics is seen to be inadequate and there is already a healthy return to the realization of the necessary place of 'natural theology'. He would never accept the arch-heresy that consigns religion to the area of Ayer's non-sense, nor would he fall into the trap of gaining religious immunity from criticism at the price of intellectual irrelevance. Likewise, while welcoming the help that psychology offers he would resist the allure of 'psychologizing the gospel' if it makes self-fulfilment the sole goal of.spiritual life. Rather he would agree with Niebuhr that 'fulfilment comes as a by-product of participating in the struggles of one's times. It cannot be sought directly or procured through therapy.'

Finally, a brief word about the man himself.

He has an extraordinary power with the young—in universities, schools, among the underprivileged and unemployed. His obvious integrity, courage, and sympathy make an immediate appeal. Entirely devoid of pomposity and any element of self-righteousness, he has the (rare) gift of making religion attractive. Never abating his own high principles, he can speak to and gain the confidence of those who hold very different views.

And, of course, it is fascinating to watch him with children—that most perceptive section of humanity. He wins their trust, he is fun, there is an immediate bond of unfeigned interest. Some of the happiest pictures are those of the bishop surrounded by a bunch of laughing children in Africa or in the East End of London. His laughter and his smile are endearing. They tell much of a man and they convey something of his zest for life with all its struggles.

As one would expect, his circle of friends is wide and diverse, but his friendship is never trivial. As someone said, 'He is the sort of man you know will never fail to remember you personally before God'. 'Amid a very busy life, needing rest badly, he will make time to join a family party.' And again, 'however long the interval between meetings with him you can take up the friendship where it left off'.

His style of life is marked by personal austerity—after all he is a member of a religious order, and one feels that inner discipline gives him strength and freedom. But this is combined with delight in the good things of life—music, art, conversation, love of the countryside and walking, and, most of all, friendship. Knowing him one realizes how true it is that often divine grace is mediated through human friendship.

Somewhere, long ago, I came across these words that have remained with me—'People have the right to expect two things and two things only of their clergy: that they will preach the Gospel and tell the truth.' However incomplete such a statement may seem at first sight, its significance grows on reflection. The obligation of this dual commitment is paramount and wide-reaching and it is far from easy to fulfil.

The greatness of Bishop Trevor Huddleston lies in the completeness of his commitment to preaching the gospel in its totality—historic, unfolding, opening up new horizons; and to telling the truth—about Africa, Britain, the world, concerning the human condition and God. And, above all, his greatness lies in the recognition that, ultimately, it is a single commitment.

Affirmative Action

JAMES THOMPSON

MY great predecessor said, 'When we have tackled race in this country we shall still be left with the issue of class.' This was not to say that class was more important, nor to say that we would solve the race issue in the near future, but to recognize that race and class are inextricably bound together, and that in this country the most deeply and historically rooted prejudice is based on class. No bishop of Stepney could fail to be aware that for most of this century the Church of England has been a minority interest among the working-class population of East London. That minority has had a profound influence on the majority, and their priests and church workers have often carried the deep respect of the people in the parishes, but church-going has remained strictly a minority pursuit.

This is a matter of profound concern, because we are committed to the gospel of Christ which transcends race and class and gender, and a true Church should pour out the Spirit of God for all to drink. 'There's no such thing as Jew and Greek, slave and free man, male and female, for you are all one person in Christ Jesus' (Gal. 3: 28). A Church which fails a class or a race is a Church which is failing in her mission, especially when it comes to the disadvantaged. When the whole of society tends to favour the strong, the powerful, and the rich, the Church should set her sights firmly on a counter bias. As *Faith in the City* poignantly asked: 'The Church seems to offer very little to people in the inner city, but surely Christianity has a lot to say?' (p. 47).

Middle-class expectation and perception dominate the Church, and nowhere can this have worse effect than in the inner cities and urban priority areas. We see in our parishes an influx of young professional people, some of whom are dedicated Christians, coming to live in East London and we have to struggle to ensure that their intellectual ability and professional skills do not reduce and force into retreat the local people, whose confidence in themselves and in the Church is only just in bud.

It was for these sorts of reasons that Bishop Trevor with others launched the Bethnal Green scheme to train local men to be local non-stipendiary ministers, to advance the local leadership in the Church through ordaining candidates who had been born and brought up in East London and who were indigenous to the local church and the area. All these years later, the priests so trained and ordained are still wrestling with the Church as it is. They have had to battle against sometimes false and nearly always too great expectations of the Church, themselves, the community, and their families. The Church finds it difficult to adjust to different forms of ministry, and it is only too easy for the voluntary priest in full-time employment to slip off the edge of the system. It is also conceivable that the making of priests is the wrong place to begin, and priority should be given to the building up of the laity to believe in their own gifts and ministry within the whole Church and in society, where they live out the Christian life. But whether we start with the clergy or the laity, it is clear that specific action and programmes have to be planned and carried out if we are to counter the institutional pressure towards a middle-class Church. When candidates go for selection, when synods are elected, when leaders are chosen, when representatives are needed in the wider Church and society, the times of meeting tend to be impossible for those at work, the style of training is often inappropriate either to the candidate or to his/her ministry, and the model of discipleship is based more on middle-class attitudes than on Christ. As *Faith in the City* puts it, 'The Church has a mind of its own. It can't see what inner city people's minds might be' (p. 106). Radical measures are needed.

In my time as Bishop of Stepney, we have tried to

concentrate upon the development of the gifts of the laity. East Londoners have often suffered at the hands of the successful, from school onwards. Time after time people carry with them a tremendous sense of unworthiness or incapacity. 'I couldn't do that', is often the first thought and feeling of many people when faced with responsibility. Yet we have seen that this is a result of false propaganda taken in with our mother's milk, and especially in the attitudes of society towards places and their people. It's hard to have self-confidence if people who live on your estate may not be given financial credit, or receive milk deliveries, and are subjected to the disastrous image-building which goes on in the gutter Press. It is hard to be confident if your memories of school are that you were useless, a failure, or a waste of a teacher's effort. A lot of love and faith are needed to reverse these feelings, and they should not be reinforced by the paternalistic care of the same old professional outsiders. East London people need to discover their own gifts, by being ministers to each other, by proper self-recognition as children of God—made in the image of God. For these theological reasons we have set up our Step-by-Step training scheme, which is a product of East London for East Londoners, and is doing the work of changing our view of ourselves. There have been marvellous revelations from people who in society's terms have little value and less recognition. 'I never thought I would be able to lead a group—I didn't even think I could take part in one.' 'I never thought I would be able to work with down and outs, let alone be left in charge.' 'I never thought I would be able to explain my own faith, let alone teach others.' 'I never thought I could do hospital visiting, let alone become a hospital chaplain.' When so much of the evidence in our lives, in our jobs, or our lack of job, in the public image of our home is damaging, then it is a real gospel joy to see people discover their own loveliness in the God's confidence which Christ can give. This has not been achieved by exams or tests, but by faith and experience—above all in the belief in the image of God in each and every person. These changes cannot be achieved on the cheap, but require a great deal of the disciples, and of those involved in the development of their talents. I sometimes think that this experience is our most important single initiative, with the widest implications not only for the Church but for an often demoralized society where unemployment, inadequate housing, poverty of life-style reduce people to being far less than God intended them to be.

As we made slow progress with Step-by-Step, I began to see that if it was bad that the Church seemed to create barriers for working-class or non-working people both in the exercising of their gifts and also in the leadership of the Church, we put up even stronger barriers to the black people who have been such a significant part of our East London community since the 1950s. This exclusion seemed even worse because so many of them had been committed and active members of the Anglican Church in the West Indies. For an account of the pain of the West Indians who came to the United Kingdom as Christians and found a very different atmosphere here, especially in the Church of England, you should read *Catching Both Sides of the Wind* by Anita Jackson. These are the words of a personal friend of mine who, when I met him, had become a senior pastor in the New Testament Church of God.

When I got to Gloucester I quickly sought out the Anglican church. I was a stranger and they offered nothing, absolutely nothing. Not that I was looking for anyone to lift me up but—I mean—a stranger in the country. Arriving with the warmth of the church I had known, I thought the church, especially the church, would have taken me in. Perhaps back home it was my local church where everybody knew everybody. I don't know. But here it was just a blank grey situation, just like the weather. Everything was cold. The people, the atmosphere. One of my first experiences was chilling. I discovered that certain pews in the church were reserved. How did I discover this? I went and took my seat, and then someone came up and politely hustled me away, drawing my attention to some name or number—I don't remember what was on the seat. And not being accustomed to English ways—you understand?—I had to think, I couldn't pick up things as quickly as they were saying them to me. I was partly bewildered. Sometimes it was days before you interpret what happened last week. When I fully realised what this person was saying to me, that the seats were reserved, I went to sit at the back. After the service nobody spoke to me. (pp. 7–8 (Pastor Ira Brookes).)

Ira points out that he realizes now that churches often treated white people like that too, but it was enough to drive him away. Ira's story can be matched by a million others. One of our local black Christians came to us from the Pentecostal Church. I had known him for several years before he told me that he had been an ordinand in the Anglican Church in Jamaica before he came to this country.

Week by week, year by year, I found myself confirming a majority of black people—young and older. On my visits to parishes I began to realize that the churches were becoming more open and friendly and more and more black people were becoming members of the Church of England and others had plucked up the courage to return. This was a hopeful and exciting sign. Yet when we elected our synods and our Bishop's Council—even in the Stepney Area—the representatives were 100 per cent white, and this in no way reflected the membership of our churches. Black people were being elected churchwarden, and very occasionally a black ordinand emerged from the parishes, but when we looked at the central councils and synods they were an all-white affair. It was at this point that the Bishop's Council and I took our next affirmative action. I invited to meet with me fifteen black members of our congregations to form a black advisory group, to consult with them about the participation of black people in the Church, to receive their own insights about their lives in society, and to explore ways of becoming a more truly representative Church. We met over a year, and then we joined the black advisory group to the elected white Bishop's Council and did a lot of sharing of our thoughts and feelings about our history and our present church life, and this strange experience of a group of black people meeting up with a group of white people. Again this was dependent upon the confidence of the participants, so that we were able to say quite painful things to each other as well as the encouraging and appreciative things we most wanted to express. I learnt from this experience that a 'token' black person puts him or her in a very exposed and difficult position, but the experience of mutual support which can come from a black group can make all the difference.

We worked on the way our system, our elections achieved their white results. It was to do with our election procedures, nomination forms, lack of confidence, and sometimes, and I think unusually, racist response. At the following elections a significant number of black people were elected to the synods and to the Bishop's Council. We have to keep working at this, because shift working and the weakness of some of our churches can keep on making it difficult to sustain, but at least we have discovered that it is possible to tackle and to achieve a raising of the profile which is so necessary if we are to transcend racial barriers. One of our own priests, Fr. Ron Farley, contributed to *Catching Both Sides of the Wind*. In a very tolerant and accepting chapter he said this:

I think that the Church as a whole, those at the top, will have to find ways of making it easier, as I said before, to get blacks to rise. It is only by seeing someone he can identify with at the top that the youngster will come forward. I'm certain that there are some black youngsters who are beginning to look at me and thinking, 'Perhaps I would like to be like Father Farley'. A six year old boy said to me the other day outside the church, 'I want to be like you'. But if they see what they think is a token priest, it won't work.

The genesis of these ideas did not just emerge from the Church, but also powerfully from the secular society. After the Brixton riots, Lord Scarman produced his historic report. In our Board for Social Responsibility in the London Diocese we saw that there was a ten-year programme. We began by looking at the changes that would be needed in the police and in society as a whole. It was only too easy to see the way in which discrimination was operating—not only in the treatment of black people on the streets, in their homes, and especially at the gate to the work opportunities, but also in the long-term effects of institutional racism iself. This was defined by the Swann Report in the following way:

The term 'institutional racism' is used by different people to cover a range of circumstances, and discussion of the extent of its influence and indeed even its existence is often both confused and confusing. Institutional racism describes the way in which a range of long established systems, practices and procedures, within both education and the wider society, which were originally devised to meet the needs and aspirations of a relatively homogenous society, can now be seen not only to fail to take account of the multi-racial nature of Britain today, but may also ignore or even actively work against the interests of ethnic minority communities. Such practices include many which, whilst clearly originally well-intentioned and in no way racist in intent, can now be seen as racist in effect, in depriving members of ethnic minority groups of equality of access to the full range of opportunities which the majority community can take for granted. Institutional racism is just as much a cause for concern as the prejudiced attitudes which some individuals may hold, since the establishment, in this way, of racism within the 'system' itself can serve to reinforce, to magnify and to perpetuate such attitudes, even where such attitudes are open to change. ('Education for All', Runnymede Research Report, 5.)

It was clear at police passing out parade at Hendon, at dining-halls in Oxford and Cambridge, in the examination of the Institute of Chartered Accountants, in the staff rooms of many schools, at business lunches, city dinners, boards of directors, council offices, at a whole range of circles in our society, that black people were not penetrating the system. The transport system, the entertainment business, sport, and the health service depend upon the black contribution, but the profile seems to have strict, even if unstated, boundaries. The reasons for this are complex, beginning from the education process so clearly demonstrated by Swann, to the great reluctance of white people to have black bosses, to the general white incredulity that black people are capable of taking senior positions and great responsibilities. These are the effects of institutional racism, and they are like a great white wall to all but the most exceptional. It was my one criticism of Lord Scarman's magnificent achievement that in one sense he let our society off the hook by not forcing us to face the reality of our subconscious racism as well as our overt more identifiable attitudes.

Our London Diocesan Board for Social Responsibility attempted to face up to these factors, and began to target the issue in key areas where the white wall seemed at its strongest. But the more we looked at the insights of both Scarman and the interim report from Tony Rampton, the more we began to understand that we had to tackle the institutional racism of the Church itself. It was no use preaching to others if we ourselves were still trapped in precisely the same bind—the growing desire to have more black participation, black appointments, and the failure to recruit, select, and train our own black leadership.

In part the slow progress was due to an apparently good motive. It derived from the belief in integration and the desire to treat all people the same. There is a telling section in the Swann report:

> The attitude of 'colour blindness', which makes no distinction between black and white pupils, is a very widespread one among teachers and it is clear that there is a substantial body of opinion within the teaching profession which firmly believes that to recognise differences between people of various ethnic origins is divisive and can in fact constitute an obstacle to creating a harmonious multi-racial society. 'Colour blindness', however, is as potentially negative as a straight-forward rejection of people with a different skin colour since both types of attitude seek to deny the validity of an important aspect of a person's identity. ('Education for All', 5.)

To treat everyone the same was both to deny the varied gifts and capacities of people from different cultural and religious backgrounds, and at the same time, because of their intrinsic disadvantages, to see such people being denied the opportunities and access to greater responsibility and recognition in society.

When I confirm black teenagers—as I rest my hands on their head I pray that God will not only send His spirit of encouragement to them, but also defend them against all the negative and hurtful experiences of life which have alienated so many of our young people into a sort of alternative culture. It breaks my heart that mums and dads who are God-fearing, law-abiding, rich in faith and grace should so often see their children being squeezed out of the opportunities which they have striven so hard to achieve for them. Not only do they meet the negative discrimination of the system, but the knife is turned in the wound by the serious racism of the tabloid Press. In my years as Bishop of Stepney, I have been sickened by the dual standards which exist in reporting disturbance, crime, and violence. The Broadwater Farm estate riot was described as 'Blacks on the Rampage' whereas the behaviour of the Liverpool fans in Brussels where thirty-nine people were killed, and indeed the behaviour of that minority of football fans, is put down to the hooligan element—not the mostly 'white' hooligan element. If there is a mugging, it is described as the work of black youths—only silence on the colour informing us that the youths were white. The riots and violence in the miners' strike and at Wapping were the work of union extremists—not *white* people. The immigration procedures, the decision to demand visas only from New Commonwealth countries, all go to feed the general perception that blacks spoil our society. I can only say that in my experience it has been our society which has spoilt the black people—conveying a stereotype which is cruelly unjustified, and by its discrimination often failing to recognize the contribution made by or the potential of many black members of our community.

So it became clear to us in the Church, as it became clear to the police, as it has become clear to the Inner London Education Authority—and indeed as it becomes clear to any concerned and caring authority who works closely with or has the benefit of the insight of black people—that affirmative action is necessary. It's not enough to be 'colour blind' and to let nature take its course. Nature, when it's human nature, has a nasty habit of treating minorities badly and tending to ghettoize them by the slow effect of passive inaction which allows discrimination to be the most successful motive.

The argument is often strongly expressed to resist 'positive discrimination' because it is unfair to people with existing rights, and because it can bring down even more anger and disapproval on the people it is geared to serve. But I have become clear that we exercise positive discrimination already in many facets of our society. I was educated at a public school which was the most emphatic and powerful expression of positive discrimination. I do see the possible divisive influence of positive discrimination, especially in a time of recession where homes, education, and jobs are all at risk and reducing in quality and quantity in sections of the community. I am convinced, however, that we have to take affirmative action—to find ways round the barriers, to take steps to avoid our own negative discrimination, to create opportunity where none can exist, to educate the gatekeepers of those opportunities. We also must encourage those black people who have given up or who are on the edge of giving up on a society which they believe is excluding them from its well-being and affluence.

I am always being told that 'they' are taking our homes, our jobs, and using up our health resources, yet every report that I have ever read has shown that black people are at the bottom of every queue—have the worst of the education system, the housing allocation, the attacks on the street, and the health provision. These facts are difficult to face up to politically, but there is no substitute for courageous analysis and action if the system is to become more fair.

One of the main benefits of our black advisory group was that it enabled me and the Bishop's Council to hear black Christians, members of our own Church, describing their experience and suggesting ways through the problems. So many white decision-makers seem to believe they know the inside story and therefore know the solution, when they have not reached the point of real communication at all. There are many examples of this. If we look at the call to reassert Victorian values, the general basis of this call seemed to be that in Victorian times parents were much more strict with their children and this enabled children to grow up with a greater respect for the authority of their parents and the morality of their society. Whether this is an accurate perception of Victorian England, it certainly has a confusing effect for the young British-born black. Many of the young black people were brought up extremely strictly. When I asked one of our vicars to explain why he was administering corporal punishment to the young black members of his congregation, he told me that he had the permission and encouragement of their parents to do so. I am not arguing the rights or wrongs of corporal punishment—although personally I regard the need to administer corporal punishment to a child as a parental failure. The point I wish to make is that while our society has turned its back on corporal punishment and moved towards a more trusting and affirming approach to children, black children have often been subject to a severely strict upbringing at home. This can be the case both in the highly disciplined Muslim home and in the Afro-Caribbean family unit. This contrast between the strict authority in the home and the more relaxed and open form of authority in the world outside can leave a child feeling socially schizoid. He can either respect passionately his parents' authority, or suppress his resentment until the inevitable time of rebellion, or he can resent the rest of society—especially the life of his mates, who seem to get everything so much more easily and are treated as more responsible. It has for a long time been a worry that black children come forward for confirmation as adolescents and then reject the faith and the Church along with the authority of their parents and society as a whole. A boy in one of our parishes was involved in a terrifying crime, and it seemed at first that he was schizophrenic. But his doctor said to me, 'No, he's not schizoid, he's not paranoid—he's a social disaster.' On the majority of occasions we see young black people loved by their parents and growing up able to cope with them and with society, but a substantial number of those who have become alienated have become so because of the total lack of consistency in their experience of family life and their wider social experience.

Another disheartening experience has been the high expectations of children and their parents of the education system, and their tremendous disillusionment when those expectations are not fulfilled. What does it do to someone who has been encouraged to believe they will be a vet, or a doctor, or a computer expert, or a chartered accountant, when they are refused interviews as a dustman or cleaner in the local hospital? What does it do to the unemployed young living within a 70p tube ride of all the brilliant glittering splendour of the West End when the options for them after their year on MSC seem to cut them off from that glittering world for ever, or at least for the foreseeable future? How can we go on stoking the appetite, when at the same time there is less and less opportunity to join the game?

These are some of the difficulties being faced by the young—many of whom have begun their life with just their mum in a rather depressing and ill-equipped flat on the nth floor of a tower block, with no dad to identify with or to feel secure with. These are not just the result of immorality or wickedness as some would suggest, they are the long-term results of deprivation, from slavery down to the more sophisticated exclusion of the present day. If this is not to be a repeating cycle, lasting through generations, then affirmative action has to be taken—especially in education and jobs, and for Christians in the Church. Indeed, if we can take such action, and be seen to be a multiracial Church at every level, we can be a sign for the wider community. This will involve us in better relationships with what we call 'black-led' churches, although I hope that name will soon not survive because we shall increasingly have black-led churches ourselves. The Christian should take the lead in restoring a sense of dignity and acceptance and affirmation to peoples who are deeply rooted in the Christian faith. This will require young and old black people to continue to call their own young to belief in the future which belongs to them, as well as to the rest of society. It is not right for us to moralize to black people, but to listen and support them in their own profound and gracious moral strengths and perceptions.

But there is a more pervasive and attainable affirmative action which is open to every member of the white community. This is not a great burden or demand or a source of guilt, or a stimulus of fear, it is rather an attitude of mind. It is easy for some of us who spend much of our time in the company of black people, who worship together, pray together, laugh together, and cry together. It is not so easy for those who have been trapped for a long time in fear or resentment, and it is not easy for those who rarely associate with or even see black people except on the television. It is the single affirmative action of pure enjoyment of people who are different from the white majority. We still have only 4 per cent of the population who are black—i.e. not white—and so it is inevitable that it is still largely in the great cities that multiracial life is the norm. But I have to say that for those of us who have the good fortune to share in a multiracial community—especially in the communities of faith—we feel deprived when there are no black people. We feel a sense of loss. It would be difficult to define what we are missing which black people present to us. It is a mixture of affection and sorrow, of joy and pain, of grace and courtesy. There is what seems like a natural capacity from God, a physical spirituality, and an exuberance which cannot be dimmed even by the difficulties. It is all the more sad when such people become alienated and sullen because of a thousand undeserved blows. In the end, we will be prosperous in spirit only when we affirm their enrichment of our lives and act accordingly.

The New Ecumenism

PAULINE WEBB

FIFTY years after Archbishop William Temple had hailed the coming together of the churches as 'the great new fact of our time', Archbishop Trevor Huddleston was suggesting that the Christian ecumenical movement had become the great old bore of our time. Admittedly, he never had been particularly enthusiastic about the various schemes for church union that preoccupied so much ecclesiastical debate in Britain during the 1950s and 1960s. He had shared Catholic suspicions about the legitimacy of the birth of the Church of South India, and had been sceptical about the Church of England's flirtation with the Methodists. But he had kept his distance from the arena of dispute, feeling no doubt that there were more urgent issues for the Church to address than interdenominational conversations. Like a fellow prophet on the Southern Africa scene at the time, Colin Morris, he would have exclaimed, 'Include me Out!'.

Yet it was initially through his African experience that Trevor Huddleston's ecclesiastical rigidity was compelled to bend before the reality of his encounter, not only with those of other Christian traditions, but with those of totally other faiths than his own, and especially with the traditional faith embedded deep in African culture. It took another missionary to Africa to encourage him to articulate this respect for traditional values and eventually even to affirm them and build Christian formation upon them. There had been a time, for example, when Christian missionaries had condemned the tribal initiation schools. But when Trevor arrived in Tanzania, he discovered that his predecessor there, Bishop Vincent Lucas, a man as devoutly and rigidly Anglo-Catholic as Trevor himself, had recognized the importance of the initiation rites in instilling into adolescent boys a pride in their inheritance and a sense of community which had a deeply religious dimension. The bishop had urged that Christians, far from deploring such activity, should learn how to build on that tradition. So it was that Trevor, who in his Johannesburg days had been ordered to excommunicate any African Christian found sending his son to a circumcision school, now in Tanzania found himself consenting to confirm boys in the Christian faith within the very context of those initiation ceremonies, the value of which he too now was coming to recognize.

This respect for the tradition of others meant a new questioning of his own traditions, and Trevor found himself theologically challenged by the issues raised in a book written by a Jesuit priest, Father V. J. Donovan, who had also worked in Tanzania. He had been living among the Masai, a people of a traditionally nomad culture. After five years of slow, unrewarded effort to gather them into the structured Church, he had come to ask, 'What are we doing, trying to institutionalise a people whose whole style of life has been one of movement and exploration? Why should the gospel be presented to them only in a Western mode?' He had written a book called *Christianity Rediscovered*, a book Trevor still quotes as a seed-bed for that new ecumenism which was to come to fruition later in his own ministry.

So it was through his encounter with the traditional cultural values of African society that Trevor Huddleston first began to question some of the traditional ecclesiastical practices of his own. He began to see the need to strip the presentation of the Christian faith of its Western accretions and to recognize that every culture has within it both that which can be affirmed and that which must be transcended by the gospel of Christ. As the World Council of Churches' Assembly at Nairobi put it in the Report on Witness:

For the sake of witnessing to the gospel of Christ, the Church is free to ground itself firmly in the culture and life style of every people to whom it is sent. Otherwise it would be like a potted plant with no roots in the local soil, rather than find life as a seed which dies to bear fruit. There is no single culture peculiarly congenial to the Christian message.

But there were deeper theological challenges to follow, when the encounter became one not only of different cultures but of different faiths, all making their claims to truth revealed from divine origins. Here again, for Trevor Huddleston the theological questioning followed the evidence of everyday experience. It was in the pluralist society of a post-Christian Britain that he became most urgently aware of the need for peoples of different faiths to learn to live in peace and charitable humility alongside one another. He became more and more seized of the importance of the doctrine of Creation, with its emphasis on the realization that all human beings are made in the image of God, an image too frequently distorted by our inhumanity to one another. It seemed to him that in Christian teaching there was a danger of too much priority being given to the doctrine of Salvation, exclusive and divisive as that can sometimes be made to sound, and too little to the affirmation that the whole world is God's world and that the mercies of God are manifold.

Characteristically, it was children who first made this message plain to him. When Trevor Huddleston became Bishop of Stepney in the East End of London, among the episcopal duties he most enjoyed were the visits to an infants' school just off the Commercial Road. When he first visited there the school was full of white Cockneys, some of whom were just beginning to learn at home the language of racial insults and the sport of 'Paki-bashing', symptoms of that xenophobia which infected extreme elements in the local community when new people began to arrive in the area from Bangladesh. Within a few years there were more Bangladeshis than white chilren in the school, along with pupils of some fifteen other nationalities. There, under a wise headmistress, children were learning from the earliest age a respect for one another's cultural festivals and a sense of belonging to one community which the bishop found a welcome antidote to the prejudices deeply ingrained in adult attitudes both within and beyond the churches. Watching Muslim and Hindu and Christian children singing together in the school assembly, 'He has you and me, brother, in His hands, He's got the whole world in His hands', and enjoying together the celebrations of Id and Divali and Christmas, he perceived with greater clarity the importance of affirming God not only as the Creator of people of every race, but also as the Creator of communities with their different cultures.

Those cultures, now coming into such close juxtaposition, could either be set on a collision course or be encouraged towards an encounter of mutual enrichment and discovery. The bishop was aware of the dangers there might be in any kind of uncritical sharing of the traditions—the danger of compromising the Christian faith (or any of the other faiths for that matter) or the danger of syncretizing distinctive faiths by suggesting that they are all mere variants of the same basic truths. But the urgency of creating a new and peaceful multi-faith community seemed to him to outweigh the responsibility of defending particular dogmatic stances, and he entered enthusiastically into the school's multi-faith celebrations.

In that East End community, there gradually emerged other signs of the ways in which human compassion could transcend traditional communal boundaries. When people back in Bangladesh were overwhelmed by disastrous floods, their families in London found English neighbours whose sympathy took typically practical form. The bishop was able to convey to the imam not only the condolences of local residents but generous gifts of money too. In the face of local, racist attacks neighbourhood solidarity groups began to be formed and protest meetings held, where the bishop was frequently regarded as the spokesman for the whole community, Christian and Muslim alike. So it was from the standpoint of a basically simple and practical inter-faith ecumenism that Trevor Huddleston embarked on the next stage of his ministry, which brought him, as he put it, to 'the crunch-point' of his ecumenical pilgrimage, breaking down any residual Christian rigidity left in him, his journey to Mauritius.

It would be easy, but misleading, to describe Mauritius as the meeting-place of many cultures. Certainly the people living in the island are of many different faiths. The majority are of Indian origin and are Hindus. The Christian, Muslim, and Buddhist communities are also represented in large numbers together with a few Sikhs and a small company of Jews. But the different communities, though living peaceably alongside one another in recent years, could hardly be said to have met in any dynamic communication. They had learned respect for one another and were interested spectators at one another's festivals, but there had been little dialogue between them. There was, however, one shared celebration which so deeply impressed itself on the new archbishop that it inspired within him the desire to foster in every way he could the friendship between the faiths which he saw as an essential ingredient in the island's peace. Once more, it was through an event rather than through an argument that this conviction was born within him.

Every year the whole community in Mauritius, whatever their faiths, shared one common pilgrimage. This was to honour the tomb and the memory of a folk-hero who had once been a village priest, Père Laval. He had come to Mauritius from France just after the Napoleonic Wars. His own people, members mainly of the French aristocracy, wanted little to do with him. They already had their own chaplains who accommodated themselves comfortably to the somewhat extravagant life-styles of their parishioners. But Père Laval made his home among the indentured Indian labourers working in the sugar fields and there lived a life of such transparent saintliness that the love of God shone through him on to everyone he met. Men and women of all faiths responded to that love and honoured the one who made it real to them. In recent years, his memory has been so hallowed that he has become, alongside King Louis of France, a patron saint of the island. The mass for his beatification was held on a high open-air site overlooking the town of Fort Louis, and was attended by over 150,000 people. Among them were Muslims, Hindus, and Buddhists whom the Roman Catholic bishop had invited to take part in the liturgy. It was a spectacular service. Following the kiss of peace, twelve boys and twelve girls opened the baskets they were carrying, releasing into the gloriously blue sky flocks of white doves, circling and calling their message of peace above the whole company. For Trevor

Huddleston, that was another of those great moments of truth, pointing him on to that search for inter-faith understanding which would not be merely cerebral but of the heart. Not for the first time, it was the children who seemed to be showing the way to that peacemaking which is the divine vocation of all the children of God.

The new archbishop's response to such a vocation was to use the enormous house he had been given as a residence to convene a conference of distinguished leaders from all the various communities of faith, and some of no faith at all. He invited them to tell one another how they would answer the question, 'What is man?' and in the light of their answers to consider together the kind of society they wanted to create in Mauritius that would enable everyone to attain the fullness of their humanity. The debate began with presentations from a Muslim business man, a Hindu doctor, a Christian bishop, a Marxist laywoman, and continued vigorously and creatively throughout the day. Sparks flew, but they were sparks of inspiration rather than of conflagration, and soon similar dialogue meetings were initiated. So, when a few months later Archbishop Huddleston received a copy of a circular letter from the World Council of Churches, seeking help in convening an inter-faith consultation preparatory to the Sixth Assembly of the World Council of Churches, Mauritius seemed to be the obvious place to hold it and the archbishop himself a more than willing host.

It was that consultation, drawing its members from fifteen different countries and seven different faith communities, that brought a global dimension to Trevor Huddleston's growing concern for inter-faith dialogue. For all of us who were there, it was one of the great life-changing events, when it was not only our minds that became intensely engaged in the process of dialogue, but our souls that were stirred by the heightened spiritual pulse of our meeting together. For ten days, in idyllic surroundings, we were able to meet at a deep level of personal encounter, sharing as much as we dared our religious resources with one another, and undermining in disconcerting ways some of the religious barriers between us, when we learned not only to share each other's prayers but to share our jokes too!

The theme of the Mauritius Consultation was 'The Meaning of Life'. Its purpose was to enable the guests who were going to attend the Christian World Assembly in Vancouver later that same year to meet one another and to give some preliminary thought to what at first hearing must have seemed to all but the Christians the somewhat triumphalist and even exclusive theme of the Assembly itself: 'Jesus Christ, the Life of the World'. So it was good for us to meet in an island where Christians were in a minority and where, under their archbishop's leadership, they had done some hard thinking about what it means to make such unique claims for the Christian faith and yet to be open at the same time to receive and respect the insights of others.

The practical, political importance of reaching that kind of mutual understanding was impressed upon us right from the start, even in the opening welcome given us by the Prime Minister of Mauritius, who acknowledged the important role of religions in promoting peace among the people. Local Mauritians were eager to demonstrate to us the daily reality of their multi-faith experience as they took us in turn to visit temples, mosques, churches, and the disturbing but profoundly moving spectacle of the Hindu Kavadi festival. There we watched young men expressing their deep devotion to their chosen deity by walking a kind of 'Via Dolorosa' carrying their own heavy yoke, with hands and chest pierced by nails and spears. Such experiences gave to the idea of dialogue a much deeper meaning than a mere exchange of words. It meant coming to terms too with the intensity of the faith commitment of others and learning how to respect it without either compromising one's own faith or patronizing theirs.

In our encounter with one another there was at first a nervousness which was especially evident when we began to consider how we could worship together. We did not feel able, nor did we want, to share one another's liturgical acts, but we agreed that a most important element in understanding the perspectives of another faith was to be aware of how people's beliefs shape the way they pray and how they perceive their personal and communal relationship with a transcendent reality. So we agreed to attend, in the fullest sense of that word, each other's daily worship, where, following a brief explanation by those participating in the liturgy, we could watch and witness what went on, and silently ponder those rituals which 'hold together the rhythm of the universe'. Very soon, in spite of all our inhibitions, I think many of us ceased to be mere observers and found ourselves absorbed in the spiritual atmosphere of what had seemed at first alien traditions. There were riches here which we felt privileged to share, whether it was being bathed in the smoke of the smouldering cedarwood and sweet tobacco of a Canadian Indian pipe of peace, or having our ears haunted by the chanting of Buddhist mantras, or being enchanted by the delicate beauty of the flowers and fruits which spoke the language of Hindu devotion. Other people's symbols spoke powerfully to our own souls. So it seemed right that, after our days of sharing, arguing, eating, living together, we did arrive finally at the point where we were unable to resist worshipping together. In our final gathering, we brought to a central table the symbols of our own faith which were most precious to us and shared our separate testimonies to what we believed to be the truth revealed to us in our Scriptures, in our traditions, and in our living experience. There was an overwhelming sense that we were standing together before a mystery too great for any of us totally to comprehend, a glimpse of that heaven beyond all our horizons, and yet made real for each of us through the graciousness of divine revelation and the humility of human response.

It was indeed an experience reminiscent of the early days of the Christian ecumenical movement, when we had at first so tentatively moved towards one another, even at the time, not so long ago, when we were still too nervous to pray together, and had discovered among our so-called 'separated brethren' forgotten heirlooms of precious worth to us all, and ancestral memories that complemented our contemporary experience. However much we protested that there was still a great difference between us and that it was safer to keep our distance from one another, we were becoming increasingly aware that we were being driven together by a love stronger than we could resist. However many failed marriage plans may have fallen into the waste-paper bins of our ecclesiastical committee rooms over the past few years, we are compelled to acknowledge now that we in the various churches are more than just 'good friends'. We have come to realize our interdependent relationship within one family, learning to live together in God's world, needing one another's insights, prayers, counsel, resources if we are to survive and if our world is to survive with us.

Now, in this latter part of the century, the wider ecumenism calls us to acknowledge that it is not solely the unity of the Church we must seek, but a global unity that acknowledges the whole earth as God's dwelling-place, where the Holy Spirit's energies have been operative far beyond the confines of the Church. We came to see that the dialogue on which we were engaged in Mauritius was not an optional extra to our religious life, but essential to our theological understanding, both of our own faith and of the experience of our brothers and sisters. As one of our participants from the Eastern Orthodox tradition put it:

The Spirit has always been at work in all humanity everywhere and at all times, giving deep experiences of reality and its meaning to people in all cultures and climes. In so far as people have responded positively to the work of the Spirit they have experienced unity with all, realization of the truth and the joyous knowledge that results from it.

Throughout our days in Mauritius shafts of light shone upon us from our shared testimonies to divine revelation found in our sacred books, witnessing to the interdependence of all life and the integrity of the whole of creation. We had glimpsed too the glory reflected in the lives of saints and mystics of all our traditions. As one participant put it, 'I have seen flashes of unconditional love here and there, and where I see it I worship, because there is the presence of God.'

There were times when we walked in dark valleys, confronting the great gulfs that still divide the human family, many of them undergirded by religious concepts, constructed with fundamental rigidity, or by political structures of injustice and oppression. There were people sitting together at our meal tables who, when they went home, would be caught up again in communities bitterly hostile to one another or totally insensitive to each other's cultural tradition or spiritual and material need. So, from the euphoria of our theological exploration and our liturgical experience, it was Trevor Huddleston who urged us to recognize that dialogue did not only mean speaking and listening with openness to one another in a common search for spiritual understanding; it also meant acting together as allies in a common commitment to work for justice and peace. No longer can any faith go it alone. We need to affirm together the God-given dignity of all humanity, especially wherever it is degraded or deprived or denied the necessities of life.

So, the Mauritius Consultation became for all of us who were there, the archbishop included, not only a meeting-place but a turning-point in our own commitment to inter-religious dialogue. We had begun to see in this whole process a sign of that 'mending of the Creation' which one of our speakers had described as sure evidence of the presence of the Kingdom of God.

It was in the last session of the Consultation at Mauritius that Trevor Huddleston announced his plans for the next stage of his ecumenical journey. He was on the eve of retirement, and declared that he intended to spend all the rest of his days in the struggle for the soul of his beloved country, South Africa. In that struggle he had now found new allies. It was, he declared, fundamentally a religious struggle. For here was a nation which claimed to base its very Constitution on an attitude of 'humble submission to Almighty God, who controls the destinies of peoples and nations' and yet which violated by its laws and actions the sanctity of human life, in a way which all people of religious faith must surely condemn as blasphemous. He pleaded that we who had now begun to talk together about our faiths should resolve to act together against this offence in the eyes of God and of humanity. To that end, he invited the members of the Consultation to meet again a year later in London at an Inter-faith Colloquium which he was organizing under the auspices of the United Nations Special Committee Against Apartheid.

So it was that several of us who had formed in Mauritius friendships which bridged our differences of faith and culture were able to meet again and renew those friendships as we carried on the dialogue a year later in Windsor. The climate was more bleak, the timetable more crammed, and our attention more concentrated, not so much on the heavenly vision this time but on earthly realities described for us in horrendous and factual detail by people present among us from South Africa and Namibia. Trevor himself was in the chair and imparted an intensity and urgency to the proceedings, which on occasion even burned into anger with anyone who tried to pass off pious platitudes or make virtuous claims for their own particular communities as being free of the evils of racism. The path to peace must lie through the way of penitence for all the wrongs that have been done in the name of every religion, for none of us have consistently practised what we have professed. But in all the faiths there are pointers along that path, and in what one speaker called 'the well-winnowed wisdoms' of the many different traditions there are words of hope for a new humanity based on mutual respect and common justice.

In the Declaration which resulted from that Colloquium we were able to demonstrate, by brief references to the distinctive doctrines of the major faiths, that though our emphases may be different, there is a fundamental and unanimous moral and religious opposition to apartheid, an opposition that led us to recommend four categories of action. First, we called the religious opposition to apartheid, an opposition that led us to recommend four categories of action. First, we called the Southern Africa, and to make the whole situation there a subject for their prayers and theological reflection. Then we called for the setting-up of more inter-faith groups who would work together both within and beyond Southern Africa to overcome exclusive attitudes and racial discrimination and to provide increased resources of humanitarian aid. Thirdly, we drew the attention of the religious world to the movements for human rights and for peace, and to the suffering of political prisoners and the oppressed. And our final call was for acts of solidarity from religious groups by their organizing boycotts, calling for sanctions, opposing arms sales, and continuing intercession with and for those victimized by apartheid or those spiritually imprisoned by their own racist ideology.

This clarion call coming from an inter-faith consultation alerted many people to the realization that religious dialogue was by no means merely an academic discipline. It could have active and even political effect. For Trevor Huddleston, it meant that, having found allies for his own cause among those of other faiths, he himself now was courted for his support in all kinds of causes sponsored by many different religious groups. The one that possibly captured his imagination most irresistibly was the building of the great Peace Pagoda in Battersea Park by the monks of the Nipponzan Myohoji Buddhist community. This had been made possible by the extraordinary generosity of their Japanese leader, Guruji Nichidatsu Fujii, once a friend of Mahatma Gandhi's, who was expressing his commitment to world peace by erecting magnificent pagodas in many of the main cities of the world. In Britain, he sought out Trevor Huddleston to be Chairman of the Friends of the Pagoda, presiding at the dedication ceremony. Among the people gathered there, Trevor could recognize many fellow pilgrims, people who had now become familiar friends—people like Sister Nara, the Buddhist nun who had expressed her opposition to apartheid by walking through South Africa and fasting on the way, and who had now embarked on her pilgrimage for peace by walking from Canterbury to Battersea for the dedication of the Pagoda.

So Trevor Huddleston has been discovering kindred souls among people of many faiths. But meanwhile he has remained much in demand as preacher and prophet to his own Christian community. Renowned Anglo-Catholic as he has been throughout his priesthood, he was the obvious choice to be invited to preach at the service celebrating the 150th anniversary of John Keble's great Assize sermon, which heralded the beginning of the Oxford Movement and the revival of the Catholic tradition within the Church of England. It was on that occasion that he confessed to having become bored with the old-style ecclesiastical ecumenism. Preaching from the same pulpit as John Keble had done in Oxford's Church of St Mary the Virgin, he gave a new context to the word 'Catholic' as he called people to pursue what he had discovered to be the new ecumenism of our time, the relationship between the faiths:

If we are truly Catholic, then universality, the proclamation that this is God's world, God's universe—is surely a prior concern to that which would make institutionalized Christianity our chief objective. It is inter-faith ecumenism—the recognition that dialogue between Hindu and Christian, Muslim and Christian, Buddhist and Christian must have priority—that should be the aim for us all in this moment of history.

That priority becomes evident to anyone who is given a glimpse into Trevor's own overcrowded diary. As Provost of the Selly Oak Colleges, now one of the main centres of inter-faith ecumenism in Britain, he is drawn into the concerns of the Islamic Centre, and the Centre for Jewish–Christian Studies, and so on, and so on. Fortunately, even with all those commitments he has yielded to persuasion to broadcast regularly in the BBC's External Services, where, in the last two years, he has undertaken two series of programmes, important because they are complementary to one another. The first was a marathon series of twenty-six short, daily 'Reflections' on each of the phrases of the Apostle's Creed. There, in classical simplicity, he outlined the main tenets of the Christian faith in all its integrity and traditional interpretation, showing how firmly he still stands in the mainstream of Catholic commitment and conviction. I mention this because it has been said that it is only those who are firmly grounded within their own faith who are also truly free to explore the faith of others. I once heard a Muslim say that 'Religion is a matter of knowing where you have tied your own camel'. Certainly, Trevor Huddleston gives clear witness that he knows whom he has believed.

That assurance gives him the freedom for dialogue, and he readily agreed to be one of a team of four people taking part in a series of inter-faith conversations, broadcast on the World Service, in which a Hindu priest, a rabbi, a bishop, and a Muslim theologian talk spontaneously about the great words of their faith, exploring the areas where they differ and finding much common ground. As they sat there in the studio talking, for example, about their concepts of the Final Judgement and of the possibilities of forgiveness, I tried to imagine some of the millions of people who would hear them over the air, and particularly some of the places where I knew people would be listening—in Israel and Egypt, in the USA and the USSR, in

India and Pakistan, in Sri Lanka and Northern Nigeria, in Beirut and South Africa—places where religion is not a cool subject of study, but a hot cause of conflict. Yet here were people of faith sitting peaceably together, hearing one another, helping one another, and having the humility to acknowledge that ultimately we all live before a great mystery and we can only share the glimpses of the truth as God has graciously given them to us.

There remain many questions to be asked. It could be said that in these inter-faith explorations we are walking in the foothills of an ecumenical volcano which could destroy many of our cherished landmarks and leave our own faith shaken to the core. Or it could also be argued that such a shaking of the foundations is a good way of ridding our understanding of all the clutter we have accumulated through the years, leaving us free to climb to heights of spiritual attainment where we shall see new glimpses of God's glory, reflected in the lives of the many who have loved and worshipped and called God by many different names. For Trevor Huddleston, that ecumenical pilgrimage means following on in the footsteps of the Christ who remains for him the way, the truth, the life of God. The way of Christ was a way of welcoming with joy every sign of faith, of hope, of love. He praised the faith of a Roman centurion, he enjoyed dialogue with a Samaritan woman, he explored truth beyond the boundaries of his own tradition and community. For those for whom Christ is their fixed centre there need be no circumference. And if, in our pushing on beyond the boundaries of our own faith and culture, we meet with those who have climbed the spiritual summit by some other route, who are we to say they have come the wrong way, or to deny that they have reached the truth?

'Will they all be proved right in the end?' Trevor was asked in one of those broadcast discussions. For answer he quoted the words of an old African parishioner of his many years ago, which can appropriately end this chapter on the new ecumenism, 'God minds His own business'.

Man of Our One World

SHRIDATH S. RAMPHAL

ONLY in recent years have I come to know Trevor Huddleston personally. Given the Commonwealth's collective resolve to see apartheid brought to an end, my doing so was both natural and necessary—which is a measure of the continuing relevance of Huddleston's perceptions and our need for his unflagging inspiration in the struggle against apartheid.

But in a real sense, I feel that I have known Huddleston all my adult life—ever since his unforgettable book *Naught for Your Comfort* appeared in 1956. The uncompromising message about the evil of apartheid which it conveyed has been a seminal factor in the growth of opposition to apartheid the world over: a message reinforced by its author's life and work over the ensuing decades. It is no exaggeration to say that Huddleston has been a channel for a particular stream of contemporary history. Thousands of readers, of successive generations, in both the First World and the Third, have had their interpretation of events in South Africa mediated, transformed, and enlightened by his vision. I count myself among that number, and feel privileged to have had the benefit of his insight at a personal level. He has not hesitated to put himself at the service of the Commonwealth in its recent initiatives to help bring peace and freedom to South Africa. The whole Commonwealth is in his debt.

But we are brought together in this anthology of tribute by the qualities of Huddleston the man—qualities placed unstintingly at the service of all with whom he has come into sympathetic contact across the world. Throughout his working life he seems never to have lost the sense of being simply a parish priest—but a priest whose parish is the world: in Langland's poetic phrase, the 'fair field full of folk'. He kept that quality as he was translated from South Africa to Tanzania to London to the islands of the Indian Ocean, and as he rose from priest to bishop and archbishop. In all these translations, he has never ceased to be the compassionate priest, whose campaigning ardour reflects his love for his fellow beings—and his anger at injustice.

The world which is his parish is not, however, a static, comfortable entity but a dynamic, difficult, global society, faced with deep-rooted problems such as racialism, poverty, unemployment and urban decay. In his life's work he has faced each of these problems, with a strength of purpose deriving from his profound religious conviction of the supreme value of each human individual, and an equal conviction of the essential oneness of all humankind. The irreversible movement of our global society during his life towards greater interdependence has made his timeless vision particularly apt for our times. He is truly a man of our one world.

It is no accident that it was a book which brought Huddleston to the world's attention. In his constant public speaking, combined with many types of written advocacy, he has never ceased to use language creatively yet practically, as a tool fine-honed for the causes he pursues. His mastery of language has been a powerful weapon. His language mirrors his personal qualities: it reflects his lofty vision united with practical awareness of how to make that vision reality; it combines cool reason and realism with the fire of passion; and above all it shows the depth of his humanity.

Indeed, because Huddleston has devoted himself to the struggle 'against' something, we must be careful not to lose sight of what he is 'for': namely, ordinary human rights, freedoms and opportunities. Over and over again his love of individuals in all their variety shines through. In this, he resembles Charles Dickens, whom he greatly admires, and like Dickens he has a special love and concern for the poorest people. Just as Dickens's incomparable descriptions of the nineteenth-century London poor resulted in substantial social reforms, so Huddleston's advocacy and activism will have enduring results, above all through his major contribution to the inevitable ending of apartheid.

Describing how poor black South Africans forcibly removed from their houses somehow rebuilt them elsewhere with scanty and shoddy materials—in language that recalls Brecht's great visions of the poor—he captures the energy and indomitable spirit of the oppressed. He was actually present in 1944 to see emerging the first of Johannesburg's shanty towns called 'Sofasonke', a name which literally means 'we shall all die together'. His life has been an affirmation that the opposite is true: that we are all destined to live together in unity on our fragile planet, regardless of racial and other differences, not only because that is the only way to survival but also, and much more, because it is right.

The sensitivity of his language as a vehicle of his humanity justifies the special contempt in which he holds the dehumanized language of apartheid and rejects the very idea of reducing the immense human variety of an African township to a mere impersonal 'location'. Equally, it would be hard to overestimate the influence of Huddleston's analysis of apartheid, and the terminology which he uses to describe it, on the way this evil is viewed by its opponents throughout the world. When he wrote in *Naught for Your Comfort* that 'hell is not a bad description of South Africa', he was thinking primarily of the fear and the frustration of those forced to live under apartheid. Since then, because of intensified repression by the regime, that description has become all the more appropriate. It was used, for example, when on Commonwealth Day, 9 March 1987, Sweden's Foreign Minister, in speaking to Commonwealth ambassadors in Stockholm, announced that Sweden could no longer wait for a lead from the UN Security Council but had decided forthwith to impose trade sanctions against South Africa because of the serious threat of the situation in Southern Africa 'not only to peace and security in the region but also to world peace'. In answer to a pro-government South African newspaper telling Sweden—and Bishop Tutu—to 'go to hell', he commented: 'Hell on Earth is what the Pretoria regime has created for the majority of its citizens. This is what is making the Commonwealth, Bishop Tutu and Sweden call for, and work for, sanctions.'

It is now a commonplace to compare apartheid with both slavery and the racial tyranny of Nazi Germany; these comparisons are found implicitly or explicitly in the pages of *Naught for Your Comfort*. In his analysis of the role which is necessary for the Church in relation to apartheid, he recalls those German clerics who were brave enough to oppose Nazism. Updating this analysis, it is now possible to see Archbishop Tutu, Dr Allan Boesak, and Dr Beyers Naudè as legitimate successors to Niemöller and Faulhaber.

And of course he has done much not only to set the terms of the debate about right and wrong in South Africa, but also to shape the instruments with which the international campaign is waged—as an external parallel to the internal struggle for freedom now rising to a climax in South Africa itself. He has been a prime mover in the whole range of boycotts—cultural, sporting, arms, and economic—and in fact made the first recorded appeal for a cultural boycott in the London *Observer* as long ago as 1954. This predated Chief Luthuli's general boycott call, which led to the formation of the Anti-apartheid Movement and the launching of the international campaign for sanctions aimed at ending apartheid. And in *Naught for Your Comfort* he· foreshadowed the sporting boycott some twenty-two years before the Commonwealth, by adopting its Gleneagles Agreement against sporting contacts with South Africa, gave a lead which was followed at the United Nations by the rest of the international community.

His anti-apartheid cause has gone from strength to strength, and has succeeded in persuading people the world over outside South Africa that apartheid is evil and should be opposed. Yet its main purpose of inspiring the shift from moral repugnance to effective concerted action against the apartheid regime has still been only partly fulfilled. And as the international anti-apartheid cause has gathered momentum, so has the scale and intensity of official repression and resistance to meaningful change in South Africa. Indeed, it is striking how little in the apparatus of power has fundamentally changed, except possibly its intensification through the imposition of repeated States of Emergency.

The laws which Huddleston saw enacted in the early days of the Nationalist government between 1948 and 1955 still remain substantially in place as the principal bastions of apartheid. The human consequences of the evil system which those laws serve and whose effects in terms of misery and deprivation he foresaw are still operative, though for 'Sophiatown' it is necessary today to read 'Soweto'. It is still the case, as it was then, that musicians and artists and writers have to be South Africa's true ambassadors, testifying to the vast reserves of creativity which cannot be quelled by suffering and subjugation, though to these ambassadors it is now necessary to add the representatives of the banned African nationalist liberation movements.

Yet there have been significant changes; above all, in the level and effectiveness of internal and external opposition to apartheid. That leaders of ecclesiastical opinion in South Africa are now also associated with the United Democratic Front against apartheid is in marked contrast to the situation during Huddleston's time in South Africa over thirty years ago—a change perhaps not unrelated to the example he set. The most significant change of all is the condition of almost permanent uprising against the iniquities of apartheid. Perhaps here, also, Huddleston's career may stand as a vector of change—because just as he was driven to pursue his Christian mission in South Africa by political means, having found that other methods were by themselves inadequate, so the African liberation movements, after some fifty years of non-violent action with little result, were forced to take up arms to counter the inherent and unyielding aggression of the apartheid state.

I want, in this contribution, to focus on Huddleston's impact on the sphere of international affairs in which we both work by considering the international, and especially the Commonwealth, aspects of the struggle against apartheid. To do so is impossible without commenting on that South African experience which is at the heart of his life's work and has inspired the particular character of his internationalism.

Huddleston has been consistently distinguished by his clarity of vision, which has enabled him to cut through superficial appearances to the essential truth. Because of the

strength and steadfastness of his moral concerns, his judgements have been pre-eminently wise and just. In his efforts to
apply moral principles in the world of political action, he
stands in the tradition of William Wilberforce, the anti-
slavery campaigner, whose memory he often evokes for
inspiration and encouragement. From the beginning of its
formulation he saw that the policy of apartheid, and the
legislation which still enshrines it, were wrong in principle—
more than that, were evil, and could not, therefore, be
'improved' or 'reformed'. This judgement, already fully
formulated by 1955, was still completely appropriate to the
circumstances thirty years later when, battered by the
renewed wave of internal protest and international pressure
generated by the so-called 'new Constitution' of late 1984, the
Pretoria authorities began to tinker with the appearances of
apartheid without changing its fundamental realities. It is still
right today.

As he has been right about the unreformable evil of
apartheid, so, in my view, he has been basically right in his
advocacy of the means by which best to combat it. His
strategy may be summed up as consisting of the arousal of
international public opinion to support the application by the
international community of the whole range of sanctions, with
the aim of putting the maximum pressure on the apartheid
regime. This is combined with a recognition that in the last
resort force is justified against a tyrannical regime which itself
daily uses force against the disenfranchized majority of its
citizens.

Huddleston is a man for our times also in his appreciation
and utilization of the power of modern communications to
inform and persuade. Through new technologies, communications (including print and broadcasting) have now transcended
geographical limitations and national divisions and made the
whole world the communicator's electronic global village. The
communications revolution is just one factor which constantly
reminds us that we live not in many worlds but in one. The
speed of modern transport making for ease of travel between
countries, the interconnectedness of international economic
life, the global commons of the environment, including the
oceans, above all the threat of nuclear destruction which

would not respect frontiers, all these factors spell out the same message of humankind's ever-increasing interdependence in our one world. Huddleston was one of the first, as early as 1955, to realize the import of these changing realities: that the world 'is progressively diminishing in size (and is therefore more conscious than ever of its need for unity)'. Such perceptions, of course, arise naturally from his vision of the oneness of humanity.

From his early campaigns in South Africa on behalf of the African communities which were being cruelly uprooted and dispossessed by the 'forced removals' of the apartheid regime, he grasped the value of gaining publicity through the news media for his stand against such injustice. While initially this publicity was little more than an attempt to make his protest heard, and was confined to a local or national South African orbit, it rapidly acquired an international dimension, as his conviction deepened of the urgent need to arouse the world to the evil of apartheid. In a logical extension of this activity, the publication of his book *Naught for Your Comfort* gave world-wide exposure to his views on racialism in South Africa and indeed to the whole issue. Having gained this high ground early on, he used it with outstanding effectiveness as a launch pad from which to project the anti-apartheid cause on the international scene over the next thirty years, so as to engage the whole weight of world opinion in helping to uproot the evil growth of apartheid.

Huddleston has defined this activity as an attempt to 'arouse the Christian conscience throughout the world', but the consciences he has aroused have encompassed many faiths, not Christianity alone. His natural oecumenism has been reinforced by his ministry as Archbishop of the Indian Ocean among the varied faiths in the islands of Mauritius and the Seychelles. The result is a belief in a multi-faith approach which is in step with contemporary developments in our increasingly multiracial global society, whose lineaments are already glimpsed in many of the world's great cities. And it is, of course, in accord with the realities of the modern Commonwealth which encompasses a diversity of races and religions across the world.

The appeal Huddleston makes is, in truth, to the universal

conscience: to that essential concern for fundamental rights of
the individual which lies at the root of the world's great faiths.
This shared human concern gives hope, first of all, that particular injustices will be righted, and among these must stand
very high the cynical and irrational injustice of apartheid,
discriminating as it does against human beings on the grounds
of nothing more than the colour of their skin, and totally
ignoring the inner man that Huddleston knows and understands
so well. Also it gives hope that we will be able to organize our
world community on the basis of human need rather than
human greed, and will abandon the selfishness of narrow
nationalisms for an international system geared to the imper-
atives of common humanity. In this perspective, Pretoria's
decaying apartheid regime appears not only as an intolerably
unjust form of social organization but also as a ludicrously
archaic one, out of touch with the forces at work on the
international scene in these end years of the twentieth century,
bound to fail in its aim of isolating black from white—as it has
already in many ways admitted—yet succeeding in isolating
itself as a state from the mainstream of international life.

He was correct in adducing that if South African newspaper
coverage had exposed injustices and embarrassed the authorities in the process, international coverage would have a
magnified impact in both respects, and would increase the
longer-term prospects for the fostering of human rights, racial
harmony, and democratic freedoms in South Africa. As with
the Soviet dissidents, the informed interest of media both
home and overseas in the South African situation has been a
force for beneficial change which those opposed to apartheid
within South Africa have welcomed, despite the increased
difficulties this has sometimes caused them. Huddleston's
experience taught him that what Pretoria cannot stand, above
all, is the truth, and to see and hear the truth of events in the
country amplified by the media across the world. There could
be no clearer evidence of this fear of the truth than the
intensified restrictions which Pretoria has placed on the media
since the renewed State of Emergency in late 1986. Unfortunately Pretoria is also capable of learning lessons: the terrible
repression, including the torture of hundreds of schoolchildren,
documented by the Detainees' Parents' Support Committee,

the UN Human Rights Commission and the International Commission of Jurists—and confirmed directly or indirectly by the agencies of repression themselves—has, owing to the muzzling of the media by Pretoria, created only muted echoes in the international community. Yet it is axiomatic that in our shrinking, interdependent world, because of people like Huddleston the truth cannot long remain suppressed.

Pretoria's persecution of the country's youth and the bravery of their resistance have a particular relevance in this consideration of Huddleston's career and example. He has always had a special love of young people and a closeness to them, which they have recognized and returned. Much of his working life throughout the world has been spent among them. He has been acutely aware of their potential for good, and has been concerned to foster it against all harmful influences, whether deriving from urban poverty, material or spiritual, in both the developing and the developed world, or from forms of official repression, seen at its worst in South African racism. One of the rich memories he brought back from South Africa is of the moment when a small boy in a squatter camp spontaneously kissed his hand before falling asleep. All the instinctive love and goodness of children the world over is in that gesture; yet Huddleston knows from experience that the same small boy, subjected to the wrong influences, can become one of the 'tsotsis'—the criminal hooligans who have their counterparts in every urban jungle. Suffering and violence can wreck young lives forever whether in Beirut or Belfast or the Rand. That is another compelling reason why the struggle for democratic freedoms in South Africa, which is increasingly being borne by the young, must be brought to a speedy and successful conclusion.

When in charge of a mission school in Johannesburg at the time of the imposition of the Bantu Education Act, he saw with typical clarity the evil inherent in this key pillar of the apartheid system, and fought against it, closing his school rather than submit to it. He is thus in accord with the students of Soweto who, since 1976, have given a lead to those struggling for freedom elsewhere in South Africa and Namibia by forcefully rejecting the degrading concept of racially separate and inferior education, rightly seeing this as a tool of oppression—in Huddleston's phrase 'education for servitude'.[1]

It is a paradox that the depth of the evil system of apartheid, and of the less organized racial discrimination which preceded it, has engendered doughty champions for truth, equality, and justice, as though the greater the wrong, the greater will be the strength of those who rise to oppose it. I am reminded of Mahatma Gandhi. He too experienced the injustice of discrimination, struggled against it in South Africa, and then returned to his own country to arouse the conscience of his fellow-countrymen and of the whole world— although Gandhi, by virtue of the accident of colour, was able to penetrate deeper into the strata of injustices which constitute the South African system.

Huddleston and people of the same company such as Michael Scott, who did so much to place the issue of Namibia in the forefront of international consciousness, deserve greater recognition than they have received, recognition which has been denied them because they stand outside the corridors of state power—a position nevertheless of some advantage because it enables them constantly to goad and chivvy those who inhabit those corridors. The metaphor is no idle one; Huddleston photographed with a petition or deputation on the steps of No. 10 Downing Street is familiar to British newspaper readers. But despite his role in the vanguard of the anti-apartheid cause, he has always made plain that the greatest champions against apartheid are not people such as himself, but those South Africans who feel its full weight and spend their lives struggling against it.

His example reminds us, however, that freedom fighters can come from any race and society. His life has been nothing if not an example of how black and white can collaborate and identify so closely that race becomes, as it truly is, an irrelevance. If all white opponents of apartheid had approached the issue with the degree of toughness and selflessness which he has shown, it would not have been so easy for those seeking to drive a wedge between the races to dismiss 'white liberals' so contemptuously. He has shown that to be white and to be liberal does not mean being soft on oneself or on those of one's

[1] Father Trevor Huddleston, CR, *Naught for Your Comfort* (London, 1956), ch. 9, 159–78.

own race. He belongs to that small group of white activists who are recognized throughout the black world, as he would wish all people to be, simply as human beings, brothers and sisters in the struggle. Clearly he has earned that right.

In South Africa and elsewhere, Huddleston has glimpsed the reality of our contemporary 'one world', which must be multiracial if it is to survive. South Africa itself is possibly the most multiracial of all societies of a comparable size, but it is a multiracial society gone wrong, in which the backward-looking apartheid regime holds a distorting mirror up to reality, showing not the unity which our contemporary situation demands but the division and separation from which our world is seeking to escape, having seen in the holocausts of two global wars the results of turning nationalism into a supremacist creed.

In its extremes of wealth and poverty, and in the different standards it applies to the whites who are mainly rich and the blacks who are mainly poor, South Africa includes both the First World and the Third. Although a son of the First World, Huddleston is a spiritual brother of the whole world, and a living embodiment of the truth that unity is possible between all human beings. In his personality and his example, he has been a bridge between the different worlds in this one world.

I am repeatedly struck by how completely Huddleston is a man of and for our times. His career is virtually contemporaneous with the changed international realities of the last four or five decades—with the emergence of the more than a hundred new nations of the Third World, increasing multiculturalism and multiracialism, and the effort to replace old systems of adversary politics, which divided the world into opposing blocs, by a new system of international co-operation expressed through genuinely global institutions that give a democratic voice to all nations, large and small alike. He has observed, shared in and acted upon the far-reaching consequences of these developments. Years before the wind of change brought independence to the countries of black Africa, he realized that South African apartheid threatened the whole concept of decolonization from minority, alien rule and was thus a challenge to the healthy development of the rest of the continent.

He correctly interpreted the Bandung Afro-Asian Conference of 1955 as 'the first indication of a shift in the balance of power'.[2] The history of international affairs over the subsequent thirty years has been in substantial part a history of the new Third World nations calling for their presence, their personalities, and their preoccupations to receive due acknowledgement within an international system still dominated by the play of great-power interests and by inherited distortions in the patterns of economic life. Preaching at Oxford in 1963, Huddleston affirmed that 'the greatest single issue confronting our generation is that of world inequalities: the plain fact that the vast majority of human beings are hungry, while the minority is affluent beyond all need'.[3] Characteristically, he translated this vision into action, working to supply food to the needy children in South Africa's townships, and in Tanzania realizing that, in Africa, to provide water could mean life itself.

The struggle against apartheid has been at the very centre of Huddleston's life and work, but it has been part of a larger struggle against oppression and poverty. It is relevant that as a member of a religious order he has taken a vow of poverty and so has completely identified himself with the poor and oppressed, wherever they are to be found. His ministries have encompassed the rural poor in Tanzania and the urban poor in London's East End, as well as the poor in South Africa. These are elements in a global spectrum of poverty which challenges the Commonwealth and the whole international community.

The contemporary Commonwealth, whose membership includes four developed countries and forty-four developing countries, is a product of historical events and particularly of changes since 1945. Because of the needs of its diverse membership, and the qualities they bring to their voluntary partnership, the Commonwealth as an organization has the role of building bridges between different nations and races which Huddleston personifies on the individual level. Support for multiracialism and international understanding, and

[2] Ibid. 251.

[3] Trevor Huddleston, CR, Bishop of Masasi, *The True and Living God* (London, 1964), 32–3.

conversely opposition to all forms of racialism and domination
of one people by another, as in colonialism, is basic to its
nature as an association which has emerged from the process
of decolonization yet which recognizes that the connections
which have been made between different peoples and cultures
can be turned to good account in the new international
situation. It follows that apartheid represents a challenge to
the Commonwealth's most fundamental beliefs, and did so
long before these beliefs were codified in the Declaration of
Commonwealth Principles in 1971. That codification itself
took place at the same time as, and partly as a result of, a
crisis caused for the association by the apparent readiness of
one of its members, Britain, to sell arms to the apartheid
regime. It is a Commonwealth characteristic to emerge from
its worst crises with its commitment to principle enhanced,
not weakened, by being put to the test. So it was in 1971, and
so it has been, and I am sure will continue to be, with other
crises posed by apartheid.

The Commonwealth feels a particular obligation to assist in
ending apartheid and bringing democratic freedoms to South
Africa because of history: until 1961 South Africa was a
member of the association. Huddleston was one of the first to
see that apartheid offered a challenge to the very basis of the
Commonwealth. In *Naught for Your Comfort*, written six years
before South Africa's policies had led to its exclusion from the
Commonwealth, he had this to say about the apartheid
regime and Commonwealth membership:

The Statute of Westminster, in conferring freedom upon the Dominions to develop towards full nationhood, conferred freedom upon
them also to remain within or to contract out of the Commonwealth.
South Africa chose the former at that time, and has continued to
abide by her choice. In so doing she has received many benefits,
economic, strategic and cultural: she has also made her material
contribution to the wealth and to the defence of the society of nations
to which she belongs. But today, with a Government determined not
only upon a republican form of state, but upon a racial policy totally
at variance with that of every other country in the Commonwealth,
the question has relevance. 'What price Commonwealth citizenship?'
or rather, 'What use?' Presumably the non-European peoples of
South Africa are reckoned to be citizens, if not of their own country,

at least of that wider society which acknowledges the Queen to be its head? But to what end? They are unable to move freely in their own land: they are unable to move out of it, even into adjacent territories acknowledging the same Sovereign. In the making of laws which restrict their freedom, they have no voice and no means whatever of making their views known. In the most essential issues which affect their liberty they have no simple access to the courts: in many such issues no access and no appeal whatever.

And he was forced to conclude: 'There is no purpose in a loyalty either to Queen or Commonwealth if neither meets your life at any point.'[4]

He was, of course, right. It became obvious to many people that if the Commonwealth did not take a firm stand against apartheid, it would fail doubly: first by failing the oppressed majority in South Africa, and secondly, it would fail itself by betraying its fundamental principles. It took six years before the contradiction of South Africa's Commonwealth membership was finally resolved, and in 1961 the other members made clear that, as apartheid and all racialism were anathema to an association based on multiracialism and human equality, there was no place for apartheid South Africa in the Commonwealth partnership.

Meanwhile, in 1959, the Anti-apartheid Movement was founded—and founded in a distinctly Commonwealth context. Though of course the reach and relevance of the Anti-apartheid Movement goes beyond the Commonwealth, it is nevertheless appropriate to point out that it was founded at a meeting in London at which the main speakers, besides Huddleston, included Canon Collins and Julius Nyerere, soon to become President of an independent Tanzania and now one of the Commonwealth's most distinguished elder statesmen.

Huddleston's leadership of the world-wide campaign against apartheid has been an inspiration to the whole Commonwealth and well beyond it. Throughout its existence, the Anti-apartheid Movement has been a spur to the official, governmental Commonwealth to keep the ultimate objective of eliminating racialism firmly in its sights, and to act to that end. This remains a valuable function today, when the total unity of the Commonwealth on the range of measures to be

[4] *Naught for Your Comfort*, 155–6.

implemented against apartheid has unfortunately not yet been achieved, and Namibia still waits for freedom from the illegal occupation regime imposed by Pretoria.

Huddleston's opposition to apartheid derives from his understanding of its destructive impact on the lives of the individuals that it seeks to dehumanize and enslave, but he has understood also the need for individuals to organize to make their opposition effective. Thus he has devoted much energy to the leadership of organizations, such as the Anti-apartheid Movement and the International Defence and Aid Fund to assist victims of apartheid inside South Africa.

The Commonwealth is also now extending its reach to provide assistance to those inside South Africa. Building on an established scheme for helping to train South African refugees in Tanzania through distance education, its Bahamas summit of October 1985 launched a broader programme, including Nassau Commonwealth Fellowships, to help South Africans disadvantaged educationally by apartheid to continue their studies in member countries. And in the broader context of national rather than individual victims of apartheid, the Commonwealth is helping to work out ways by which the international community can assist the Southern African front-line states which suffer from the regime's campaigns of destabilization and outright aggression against its neighbours.

Huddleston himself, during eight years as a bishop in Tanzania, saw how the cost of the freedom struggle was being borne by those who could least afford it—the people of Africa themselves and their countries battling with problems of poverty and development—for thousands of refugees were pouring across the border into his diocese of Masasi, as a result of Mozambique's ultimately-victorious struggle for liberation. In recent years Mozambique has had further to endure the trauma of South African-supported rebellion. The front-line states have never stopped sharing the burden of South Africa's freedom struggle.

There has been an almost symbiotic relationship between the Anti-apartheid Movement and the Commonwealth in matters relating to its stand against apartheid, but the relationship has never been closer than in recent years, when the Commonwealth has redoubled its efforts to play a constructive part in bringing about the elimination of apartheid. With his publicizing skills, it was inevitable that Huddleston would be closely associated with the Commonwealth's programme (which stems from the New Delhi summit of 1983) to counter South Africa's pro-apartheid propaganda. When the Commonwealth Secretariat and the United Nations Centre Against Apartheid held a joint conference on the subject in May 1985, he was one of the principal speakers. And when, pursuant to its Nassau Accord, the Commonwealth decided to send the Eminent Persons Group on their 'Mission to South Africa' (as their published report was called), he was naturally one of the individuals invited to put his views to the Group. I recall vividly the force with which he put two main propositions before the Group: that apartheid was fundamentally evil and therefore could not be reformed, and that the time for action was now—the Group should brook no delaying tactics on the part of Pretoria.

There is a story he recounts which adds weight to his viewpoint. It tells how the Secretary-General of the ANC and a small delegation of black South Africans come to London to plead the case for restitution of citizenship and land rights before the British government. The government is described as listening sympathetically, then communicating with the South African government, commending the deputation and their presentation of their case. There is a sting in the tail of this story, however, when it is revealed that the ANC leader was actually Sol Plaatje in 1919, appealing to Prime Minister Lloyd George, who then wrote to General Smuts. Nothing could illustrate better how little has changed in South Africa, and why the pressure for change there is now irresistible.

The continuity is one not only of need but of response. Through all the years of oppression, the leaders of South Africa's black majority have never given up the struggle. In a special way, Huddleston embodies the continuity of that cause, and its example of transcending all barriers of race in the face of Pretoria's racism. When he went to South Africa, he came to know one of the members of Sol Plaatje's delegation to London. And when he worked in the early 1950s against the imposition of the Bantu Education Act and the Group Areas Act, which authorized the destruction of

Sophiatown, he stood shoulder to shoulder with the young lawyers Oliver Tambo[5] and Nelson Mandela,[6] now respectively the ANC President and South Africa's most widely recognized leader imprisoned for over two decades. At the National Convention to approve the Freedom Charter on 25 June 1955, Huddleston was not only present but was given the movement's highest award, a distinction he had to receive alone because the two other recipients, Chief Luthuli—later the 1961 Nobel Peace Prize winner—and Dr Yusuf Dadoo—the South African Indian Congress leader—were restricted or detained by the Pretoria regime.[7] Huddleston has known successive generations of leaders of South Africa's liberation struggle on terms of the closest friendship. Even in the mid-1980s, in the upsurge of defiance triggered off by the imposition of the so-called new Constitution (which still excludes the black majority from the franchise), Bishop Tutu used a prayer written by him at the funerals of people killed by the regime, to try and calm the anger of protest.[8] He is at one with the natural leaders of South Africa's non-white peoples because he is at one with their struggle.

It is hardly surprising therefore that Huddleston's arguments were listened to with great attention by the Eminent Persons Group, as they knew that a whole lifetime of experience was summed up in them. His advice proved to be entirely appropriate and correct. The Group was also able to judge on its visits to South Africa how durable were his assessments of South African realities—for example, the South Africa of extreme contrasts which he had described in *Naught for Your Comfort*, where wealth was white and poverty was black, emerged clearly from their Report.[9] They concluded that 'the cycle of violence and counter-violence has spiralled and there is no present prospect of a process of dialogue leading to the establishment of a non-racial and representative government'; also that 'overall the concrete and adequate progress looked for in the Nassau Accord towards the objectives of "dismantling

---

[5] Ibid. 139–44.
[6] Mary Benson, *Nelson Mandela* (London, 1986), 57–8.
[7] Ibid. 66. [8] Ibid. 241.
[9] The Commonwealth Group of Eminent Persons, *Mission to South Africa: The Commonwealth Report* (London, 1986), 23 ff.

apartheid and erecting the structures of democracy in South Africa" has not materialized'. A key part of their conclusions was that a racial conflagration—'what could be the worst bloodbath since the Second World War'—was the certain prospect not only for South Africa but for the whole region unless the cycle of violence was broken.[10] I believe that in these conclusions the Group kept faith with Huddleston's vision; that, indeed, that vision helped substantially to make the Group's conclusions possible.

The Report of the Eminent Persons Group is part of the Commonwealth's answer to the question Huddleston raised so long ago, of whether loyalty to the Commonwealth touched the lives of Africans in South Africa in any way. It exemplifies the effort which the Commonwealth has been making for nearly three decades—not always successfully and not always with sufficient unity and conviction—to fulfil its obligations to all the people of South Africa and thus to live up to the ideals expressed in the Declaration of Commonwealth Principles. It has been shown repeatedly that apartheid poses a challenge to everything the Commonwealth stands for. That remains true today. That is why the Commonwealth faced a crisis of unity at the time of the London Review Meeting in August 1986, when there were serious differences in the association over the level of sanctions to adopt against the apartheid regime, and why the Commonwealth tried so hard to overcome these differences, which have not yet been fully resolved.

To be able to praise, in this tribute to Huddleston, someone who has consistently chosen the right path, is such a rare privilege that it is necessary to beware of sinking into self-satisfaction or complacency. Any such complacency, however, is easily dispelled by a realistic assessment of the gap which still remains between the present situation in South Africa and the goal of freedom for all its people. The Commonwealth is determined, though, to face the challenges which remain and to overcome them one by one until the ultimate goal is reached. I believe that it has already gone some distance towards answering the question of how closely it touches the lives of South Africans. All opponents of apartheid were

[10] Ibid. 138–41.

greatly encouraged by the statement of Oliver Tambo, the ANC leader, that, in the eyes of black South Africans, the country had never really left the Commonwealth. The time must not be too far distant when a free South Africa, a South Africa freed from apartheid, can again take its rightful place in the association.

One of Huddleston's most valuable qualities is his righteous anger. He is angry about many things—about the blight with which apartheid has withered so many millions of lives, about the snail's pace and the cosmetic nature of change in South Africa, about the failure of those who are most powerful in the international community to take effective action, as they can and must, to force Pretoria to abandon apartheid. As we celebrate Father Huddleston's seventy-fifth birthday, we will pay him the most appropriate homage if we share something of his anger. It will not be difficult to do so if we recall that he was born in 1913, the year of the supreme injustice of the Native Land Act which consigned South Africa's black majority to their country's marginal lands, and that the years of his life coincide almost exactly with the life of the independent South African state, which came into being simultaneously with the injustice of the deprivation of the few civic rights of the black majority—and has since compounded that injustice many times over. Even at that initial nadir of injustice, however, the light of hope and humanity refused to be snuffed out; for in 1912, two years before the formation of the Afrikaners' National Party, black South Africans borrowed a title from that other freedom movement, the Indian Congress (it was one world even then), and organized themselves in the South African Native National Congress, later the ANC, the first organization dedicated to the restoration of freedom and justice for all South Africans. There is indeed cause for all who care about these aims to be angry that their achievement is so long overdue. It is time now for freedom and justice to triumph.

'Nobody Knows Who I Am Till the Judgement Morning'

ROWAN WILLIAMS

TREVOR HUDDLESTON'S name stands in the forefront of the names of those who have understood that the experience of racial struggle in Africa, and especially in South Africa, is not something different in kind from what goes on in the 'advanced' societies of the West: so much is clear from his work and witness in the UK, as Bishop of Stepney, and as an active and activating presence in so many anti-racist movements for nearly twenty years. It is appropriate, then, to celebrate such a man by attempting a sketch of what it is that unites the various forms of racial injustice, and what exactly it is that the Christian Church's reflection has to bring to bear on what is becoming a more, not less, critical situation in our own society and in the world at large. This means attempting a definition of 'racism' and beginning the task of theological critique. It may be thought that this is both too elementary and too ambitious a project—too elementary because we know what racism means, and it is a waste of time to devote more words to it (rather than getting on with practical responses); too ambitious because it requires a degree of historical and sociological expertise, personal engagement, and innovative theological power that few people—certainly not white academics at Oxford—possess. None the less, the effort seems to be worthwhile, however inadequate its results. I am aware both of a continuing confusion about the word 'racism' itself, and of a rather uncertain quality to some of our theological responses—as if the appeal to a liberal sense of human equality would do the job for us; if this essay can suggest a few clarifications in both these areas, it will not have been wasted.

It is still common enough in Britain to assume that 'racism' is essentially a word that refers to *attitudes*. If we hear statements like 'Britain is a profoundly racist society' or 'the Church is a racist institution', we are inclined ('we' being a large part of the white population—and even the black population—of the United Kingdom) to be baffled or angered. It sounds as if someone is accusing the nation or the Church of racial prejudice, of disliking or despising black people; and it is reasonable enough, in many cases, to reply that we do *not* have such attitudes, that we do not consider black people inferior or treat them differently. This *may* be a self-deceiving response, but it is not always so; and a person in Cornwall or Cumbria or Norfolk may genuinely not know what could possibly be meant by being told that she or he lives in a 'racist' environment. The sense in which it is true that they do so needs careful statement.

Two things compound confusion here, I believe. One is the common radical elision of 'racism' and 'Fascism', manifest in the names of several anti-racist pressure groups, as if racism were simply a function of a particular kind of authoritarian politics, classically represented by the Third Reich and its allies. Several points need to be made about this. German (not Italian) Fascism did indeed rest upon a commitment to the superiority and glorious historical destiny of a particular variety of Caucasian peoples; but if it is suggested that racism entails commitments like this, it is manifest nonsense to say that ours is a racist environment. The running together of racism and Fascism as a single compound iniquity is—you might say—a subtle device of the devil to prevent us grasping the *real* dangers of these phenomena. If we suppose that racism *is* the crude mythology of the *Herrenvolk*, and if we suppose that Fascism *is* the overt and brutal suppression of non-Caucasians, we are dangerously narrowing our political imagination, making ourselves less capable of seeing and understanding racism in the structures of societies, and

Fascism in a pervasive and often elusive trend towards centralized authority, the disenfranchizing (effectually if not openly) of a working population, and the militarization of a national economy. Of course, there are neo-Nazi groups around, which need to be resisted strenuously: the fact that ours is a society that tolerates them, and that our police forces in some areas can give every appearance of lukewarmness in enforcing the law against them, is scandalous. But that is where the heart of the racist problem lies—in those who *know* they are not 'Nazis', but are culpably unaware of the nature of their society as a whole. If racism were simply a problem about the National Front, it would be a good deal easier; as it is, the glib identification of racism and Fascism provides an excellent alibi for the powers that be, because it is so obviously absurd. 'If *this* is racism, of course we're not guilty of it.'

Racism, then, is not the same as overt supremacist ideology. But here the second confusing factor comes into play. Racism is not overt, so it must be hidden; it must be buried deep in our consciousness, needing to be excavated by suitable means. Part of this is rooted in a familiar kind of liberal self-punishment: my good will alone does not secure change, and so perhaps it is impure and in need of challenge and refinement. The popularity of 'racism awareness' as a theme for training events inside and outside the churches, and the development of a whole philosophy of concealed racism, reflect this sort of response. It is not wholly to be dismissed, though it has come in for some fierce criticism from writers both black and white:[1] there are, for most of us, areas of unexamined prejudice and fear that are none the worse for being looked at. But what is there here beyond the inducement of further white guilt exposing itself to further black anger? If 'racism awareness' suggests that the solution lies in improved consciousness of one's own imprisonment in negative attitudes, it risks making the whole issue private, or even seeing it as

---

[1] For a particularly savage attack, see A. Sivanandan, 'RAT [Racism Awareness Training] and the Degradation of Black Struggle', *Race and Class* 26: 4 (1985), 1–33. On some of the cultural difficulties involved in 'selling' white middle-class techniques of group work to the black community, David Moore has some barbed remarks in 'Liberty to the Captives', *Voices from the Urban Wilderness*, ed. P. Barnett (Bristol, 1984), 36.

primarily a question about white people's minds rather than black people's lives.

To a lesser degree, the same thing holds for the pouring of energy into campaigns for the sanitizing of children's reading. There is no doubt that, *given certain cultural circumstances*, a book such as *Little Black Sambo* will reinforce models of black people as alien, mildly comic, or mildly alarming. But since reading is and ought to be—for adults as well as children—an experience in which acceptable and unacceptable images and proposals crowd upon us together, there is never any real possibility of wholly 'safe' literature. There are circumstances in which we ought to be *very* wary of exposing children to certain images; but if we are really interested not in preserving a child's supposedly innocent awareness but in an effective change of relations in society at large, a degree of sceptical detachment about the literature issue will probably do no harm. The banning of a 'racist' book in an area—a country—in which black people are systematically disadvantaged is not going to get us very far (any more than a ban on alcohol advertising at Christmas would reduce the menace of drunken driving in a context in which seasonal alcohol abuse is taken for granted). The priorities should be (and happily often are) the reinforcement in newly written literature of the normality of racial pluralism, and, still more, education in understanding a social history and a social practice which has built racial disadvantage into itself (part of which will, of course, involve the explanation of how literary and narrative and pictorial stereotypes are created).

If these confusions—racism as overt supremacist ideology and racism as secret sin—are set aside or at least put in context, how are we to define the term? The World Council of Churches produced in 1975 a brief report on a consultation dealing with 'Racism in Theology and Theology against Racism', in which they suggested seven marks of the presence of racism;[2] these provide an unusually clear picture of what we are talking about.

---

[2] *Racism in Theology. Theology against Racism. Report of a Consultation* (Geneva, 1975), 3–4. For further discussion of the definition of racism, see the entry on the word in F. Ellis Cashmore (ed.), *A Dictionary of Race and Ethnic Relations* (London, 1984), 225–9.

Racism is present whenever persons, even before they are born, because of their race, are assigned to a group severely limited in their freedom of movement, their choice of work, their places of residence and so on.

Racism is present whenever groups of people, because of their race, are denied effective participation in the political process, and so are compelled (often by force) to obey the edicts of governments which they were allowed to have no part in choosing.

Racism is present whenever racial groups within a nation are excluded from the normal channels available for gaining economic power, through denial of educational opportunities and entry into occupational groups.

Racism is present whenever the policies of a nation-state ensure benefits for that nation from the labour of racial groups (migrant or otherwise), while at the same time denying to such groups commensurate participation in the affairs of the nation-state.

Racism is present whenever the identity of persons is denigrated through stereotyping of racial and ethnic groups in text books, cinema, mass media, interpersonal relations and other ways.

Racism is present whenever people are denied equal protection of the law, because of race, and when constituted authorities of the state use their powers to protect the interests of the dominant group at the expense of the powerless.

Racism is present whenever groups or nations continue to profit from regional and global structures that are historically related to racist presuppositions and actions.

Racism is here presented with exemplary lucidity and comprehensiveness for what it is, an issue about power, decision, and definition. As Ann Dummett points out, in what is still one of the best available studies of racism in the UK, it is in this respect closely akin to other sorts of disadvantage, 'one kind of injustice among many. The very poor in England are insulted for their poverty, bullied by officials, exhaustively interrogated before they can get free school meals or a clothing allowance for their children, placed under intolerable strains and then told they are inadequate when the strains are too much for them';[3] though racism compounds the injustice by assuming the right to tell people (including British citizens)

---

[3] Ann Dummett, *A Portrait of English Racism* (London, 1973), 2nd edn. (CARAF Publications, 1984), 150. On the interrelation of race and class dominance, see Philip Mason, *Patterns of Dominance* (Oxford, 1970).

where they can live, the right to deport those deemed
undesirable. And it is a simpler matter to identify the victim
because of accent or skin colour. But the oppression of the
poor and the oppression of the ethnically distinct have in
common one central feature picked out by Ann Dummett at
the very beginning of her book:[4] the oppressor makes the
claim to *tell you who you are*, irrespective of your intention, will,
preference, performance. Only certain people have the right to
construct an identity for themselves; others have their roles
scripted for them. Although all human beings are liable to be
drawn into the fantasy lives of others, individual and
collective, racism and, in a rather different way, class injustice
allow fantasy to be acted out in reality: with these people we
really can impose the roles we fantasize because we have the
political or economic power to determine the options of the
powerless and, in some measure, the very *self*-perception of
the powerless. Many of the Victorian poor adopted the images
offered them by the wealthy, as even the barest acquaintance
with nineteenth-century fiction will show. Many of the
disadvantaged in our present society will at some level do the
same, accepting the social estimate of their own worthlessness
—if not overtly, then in forms of behaviour that express
'worthlessness', violence or extreme passivity or the abuse of
the body by alcohol and other drugs. And there are still
sections of black communities willing to accept white definition
into their own imagining of their humanity.

All the signs of racism identified in the WCC document take
for granted this same fundamental privation, the taking away
of a right to determine the conditions and possibilities for a
specific variety of human living, of the freedom to define
oneself, as person or as community, of the freedom to
contribute as one wishes and needs to the *public* life, the shared
conflict and conversation that shapes the wider community of
a state. Ann Dummett comments on the 'Black Power'
phenomenon of the late 1960s and 1970s that it makes one

[4] Dummett, op cit. 55–8. A recent work which pinpoints the 'intentional'
factors in various forms of disadvantage—i.e. the processes of creating roles
for the disadvantaged, over and above the economic elements involved in
these structures—is Arthur Brittan and Mary Maynard, *Sexism, Racism and
Oppression* (Oxford, 1984); see esp. 214–17.

central statement: 'I shall tell you what I am. Black Power can
mean a hundred different things, but it is always supported by
this basic significance.'[5] This statement has commonly been
interpreted as implying an unrealistic and destructive separatism:
white critics are quick to say that the aspiration to say 'what I
am' independently of other communities and persons is a sign
of infantile disorder, neurosis, and to talk of 'black racism'.
But this is a giveaway. White domination has been built on the
assumption that whites may say what they are independently
of the needs and *reality* of other groups, who are built into
white self-definition. The refusal of that definition is not a bid
for an unreal autonomy—though it may need and use
violently separatist rhetoric, and some, black as well as white,
may be deceived by that rhetoric—but a necessary move in
challenging one human group's existing practice of 'saying
what they are' in just the infantile and disordered way they
are so eager to condemn. And if 'black racism' unquestionably
exists, as a matter of structural oppression or discrimination
exercised between black groupings, it is *not* to be confused with
'black consciousness' or 'Black Power' movements in their
hostility to white culture.

If a dominant culture (linguistic, ethnic, sexual) does in fact
work by assuming the right of definition, it is hardly
surprising if the reaction is, 'We don't need you to tell us what
we are'. Certain kinds of separatism are necessary to highlight
the reality of a difference that has been overridden by the
powerful conscripting the powerless into their story. From
being a domesticated curiosity, whose strangeness or otherness
is defused by absorption, functionalized by the dominant
group, the disadvantaged group must become *real* strangers,
with a life manifestly *not* like that of their former masters.
They must acquire or re-acquire a kind of shared secret, a
distinct human 'dialect' bound up with a distinct group life.
Oppressed groups have often done this even in the midst of
their very oppression—secret languages, covert religious
rituals, a subterranean scheme of authority relations within
the group. Liberation has something to do with the presenting

[5] Dummett, op. cit. 57. A helpful guide to the evolution of black
consciousness movements is offered by Chris Mullard, *Race, Power and
Resistance* (London, 1985).

and owning in public of this reality of shared life behind and
beyond the roles defined by the power-holders; and this means
an accentuation, not an erosion, of difference—which is why
racial justice and racial equality do not begin with 'treating
everyone alike'.

The liberal assumption that 'treating everyone alike' is the
answer rests on a view of human nature which is deeply
problematic. It assumes that there is a basic 'inner' humanity,
beyond flesh and skin pigmentation and history and conflict,
which is the same for all people. But human existence is
precisely life that is lived in speech and relation, and so in
history: what we share as humans is not a human 'essence'
outside history, but a common involvement in the limits and
relativities of history. The only humanity we have is one that
is bound up in difference, in the encounter of physical and
linguistic strangers. Of course there is a sense in which we are
all *biologically* the same; but the whole point is that properly
human life is not confined to biology, to the level of 'species-
being', as it has been called. It is unavoidably 'cultural',
making and remaking its context, and so unavoidably diverse.
When great stress is laid upon our oneness 'under the skin',
there is always the risk of rendering that as 'this stranger is
really the same as *me*'—which subtly reinforces the dominant
group's assumption of the right to define. The norm is where I
or we stand. This risk is one reason for looking very hard at
the goal of 'treating everyone alike'. It represents the worthy
and correct commitment to avoid discrimination that overtly
disadvantages or distances the stranger; but it can fail to see
the prior need to allow them to *be* strangers.

But the liberal's anxieties have some point. Careless talk
about proper distances, allowing the independence of another's
story and perspective, and so on can be costly, for at least two
reasons. The 'licensing' of difference, even the practices of
positive discrimination, on the part of a dominant group will
fail to move things forward if it is simply a concession that
does not alter the basic realities of power in the 'public spaces'
shared by dominant and subordinate groups. Or, in plain
English, the dominant group's own possibilities have to
be affected by this process if there is to be real change.
Otherwise, you have the situation classically exemplified in

the black 'homelands' of Southern Africa: grants by the dominant group to sustain a fictionally distinct economy, with special opportunities for aspiring black entrepreneurs in their 'own' setting—and a regressive interest in picturesque tribal tradition for its own sake. Nothing substantial has changed.[6] This leads on to the second point. It is actually impossible in any imaginable future world that human groupings should be able to pursue their goals in total mutual independence: 'separate development', by whatever name, is a fantasy in a world of interlocking economy (and ecological crisis). The challenge then is how human beings unashamed of their difference and strangeness are to work with the constraints of this environment—how are they (to use a fashionable term) to discover a common 'human project'? The liberal rightly sees that a world of encapsulated group identities pursuing self-defined goals is a ludicrous and dangerous idea, and insists on some kind of assumption that the human race can acknowledge a shared context and a shared goal—and that at once implies, if it is taken seriously, an effort towards shared 'power' in the world; which in turn involves certain groups facing the potential diminution of the power they actually have.

These remarks are not original or profound: they reflect what has been variously acknowledged by the Brandt Report and explored imaginatively by writers like Schumacher and Capra. However much these explorations may be Utopian dreams, I think it is important that any discussion of racism should carry the recognition that the problem of power and its sharing is a global one. The issue of racism and the combating of racism in this country and its churches, the problems (so wearyingly routine sometimes to those practically involved, black and white) of educational justice, serious attention to even the most elusive forms of disadvantage, vigilance about the methods and assumptions of law enforcement—all this is part of what even the least Utopian must see as the facing of a world-wide crisis about the distribution of power. That it *is* a crisis should be clear enough once we start thinking about the chaotic economies of poorer nations, at the mercy of markets

---

[6] See e.g. David Sheppard, *Built as a City: God and the Urban World Today*, 2nd edn. (London, 1985), 188, on the dangers of replicating white patterns of inequality within the black communities.

elsewhere, the alarming pressures of drought and famine in Africa, in countries without (or denied) the resources to deal with them, and the way in which East–West conflicts poison and intensify the wars of the Third World (not least through the atrocity of the arms trade). If South Africa dramatizes in its internal life the racial conflict elsewhere, its external relations with Mozambique equally sharply crystallize the far wider problem of First World–Third World relations in all these aspects. Defining racism ought to introduce us to the larger task of defining this human crisis overall.

2. POWER AND THE GOSPEL

The Christian response to these issues can appear banal. The issue of racism is not much illuminated by the bald statement that all human beings are equally in the image of God and so deserving of 'equal treatment'. The belief in equality before God coexisted happily for centuries with all kinds of practical injustice (slavery, the oppression of women, and so on). It is probably right to see *theories* of racial inequality as a product of the post-Renaissance period, as new relations with 'subject peoples' required rationalization—a rationalization commonly provided in the new language of 'primitive' and 'civilized' peoples, further compounded by theories of physiognomically conditioned differences in levels of intelligence, evolving in the heyday of scientific expansionist confidence in the nineteenth century. The problem, in other words, is not directly with the Christian view of human nature. It is how to prevent that view turning into an impotent abstraction in the face of the development of new power relations and the obstinacy of old ones. And this will involve an attempt to theologize in a way that does not seek to avoid the particularities of human history and yet can act as a point of judgement and hope within that history.

Christianity should have no quarrel—quite the contrary—with what has been said about the unavoidably cultural character of human beings. The Christian faith is, after all, a network of communal relations before it is a theology, and it claims insight into the truth of the universe only by way of engagement in a specific ethnic history (that of the Jewish

people) and in the new 'nation' or 'race' of those who come to
be in Christ. It is, as is so often pointed out, concrete and
narrative in its account of itself and its origins. It is not that
we *begin* with a belief in human equality and then try to work
it out (or not, as the case may be), but that the inner logic of
life shared with others in relation to Jesus of Nazareth pushes
the community outwards to 'the ends of the earth'—with all
the implications that has for a vision of the comon goal or
project of the human world as such. *All* may now be invited to
share the hope of and the work for the Kingdom; all may find
their humanity defined afresh in this project. All therefore can
be delivered from the claims to finality of the definitions given
them by their social and political context—as Paul suggests in
1 Cor. 1: 26. Those without tangible status are given standing
by God, who thereby demonstrates *his* freedom from the social
order and the relations it takes for granted. It may be too that
those with *anomalous* status in society, those whose actual
influence cannot be recognized fully in the terms of the
dominant pattern (the freed slave, the independent business
woman), are drawn in to such a group.[7] In any case, the point
is that the society of the Church in its origins creates
considerable tension with the society around because it will
not take for granted (even if it will not often challenge head-
on) the finality and authority of the socially prevailing
accounts of status and power.

The more Christianity ceases to be a distinctive communal
life to which adult persons choose to commit themselves, the
more this tension is eroded. The more 'natural' it is to be a
Christian, the more Christianity will be assimilated to what
seems 'natural' in society—a process already visible within
the New Testament itself, in the fairly well-established
churches to which the letters to Timothy and Titus belong.
There is little point in longing romantically for the rediscovery
of a purely 'sect-like' Christianity, because that would be to
ignore the historical inevitability of second-generation problems,
the transmission of belief through upbringing rather than
preaching, and so on. But we can ask at least what this

[7] See, for discussion of these and other possibilities, J. H. Elliott, *A Home
for the Homeless* (Philadelphia and London, 1981), and Wayne Meeks, *The
First Urban Christians* (New Haven and London, 1983).

definition of human beings in relation to the Kingdom
actually means, what it is that gives the Church *some*
continuing point of reference beyond what either it or the
society around it takes unreflectively for granted. In what is
left of this essay, I want to point to two aspects of Christian
language that may represent something of this abiding point
of reference, and may shed some light on the problems we
have been looking at in the first part.

(*a*) For Paul, the Church as 'body' is a system of
interdependence: no one part can be reduced to a function of
another (defined in terms of another) and no part can claim to
subsist in its own right (1 Cor. 12). And this is not simply a
static observation on the underlying structure of the community,
but acts as a principle of judgement and direction in its life. In
1 Cor., Paul is chiefly concerned with relativizing the claims of
the charismatics; but earlier, in 1 Cor. 10, as in Rom. 14, he
deploys it also against those who assume the right to set
standards of behaviour in disputed matters. There are those
who are persuaded (rightly, Paul thinks) that food regulations
are of no significance; but such people may see their 'right' to
eat anything as a kind of status-conferral, carrying with it the
power to prescribe to others the abandonment of their
traditions. This is as bad as the tyranny of (presumably
Jewish-Christian) conservatives, and is a fertile seed-bed for
resentment and division. Paul sharply reminds the anti-
traditionalists that Christ died for the Jewish-Christian
conservative too (Rom. 14: 15), and directs all to the central
principle of 'building up' (Rom. 14: 19, 1 Cor. 10: 23). Action
in the Church must be regulated not by abstract rule but by
the goal of reinforcing and affirming the other believer in such
a way that the community overall is affirmed and strengthened
and moved on towards the Kingdom. In other words, my act
must be a *gift* for the deepening and strengthening of another's
faith (and I must be open to receive such a gift likewise); it
cannot ever be a manifestation of my status or 'liberty' or
'maturity' as a thing in itself. Paul makes it generally clear in
word and practice that one's action can at times be a gift in
the form of a challenge (Gal. 2: 11 ff.): because it is a
particular *kind* of community that is being built up, there are
divergences that cannot be tolerated—such as the exclusive

and rigorist policy of some of the very Jewish Christians Paul elsewhere defends. Compromise here is *collusion* with what is actually destructive of the other person and of the whole group's integrity.

On the one hand, then, it is foolish and destructive to sneer at the forms of devotion others cling to, however 'weakly' or irrationally. If you want this to change, you must not assume *you* have the right to decide for change, but should ask, How can I come to be *trusted* by the other in such a way that we can both be changed? On the other hand, it is equally foolish and destructive to say, I will tolerate this or that assertion of right and status, whatever the cost to those victimized and bruised by it. That leaves no real opening for change—repentance—at all. Both perspectives take it wholly for granted that change, constant conversion, is central for the Christian community, and that no one group has the right to define unilaterally for others what this is going to mean. There is no alternative to the work of mutual trust—which already implies a certain relinquishing of power. The hope is for a shared and reciprocal *empowering* for growth towards the Kingdom.

This is something like the insight of the desert father who said, 'Our life and our death is with our neighbour'.[8] It is not without each other that we move towards the Kingdom; so that Christian history ought to be the story of continuing and demanding engagement with strangers, abandoning the right to decide who they are. We shall none of us know who we are without each other—which may mean we shan't know who we are until Judgement Day. In the words of the spiritual movingly quoted by Sandra Wilson at the end of a lecture on 'A Black Theology of Liberation', 'Oh nobody knows who I am / Till the judgement morning'.[9] And this should also be related to the great wound and humiliation in Paul's own experience, the growing rift between the Church and the Jews. In Rom. 11, he turns on the Gentile Christians with passion: they think Israel has been rejected to make room for them, but in fact their welcome into God's people is only an episode in

[8] Attributed to St Antony the Great; B. Ward (trans.), *The Sayings of the Desert Fathers* (London, 1975), 2.
[9] *Anglicans and Racism: The Balsall Heath Consultation, 1986* (Board for Social Responsibility, 1986), 15.

the greater history of God's reclaiming of all who have been his own. There will be no Gentile salvation without the ultimate reconciliation with the Jews: 'not without each other', once again. The Church's alienation from the Jews is precisely the kind of separation that is necessary for a final unity that is more than trivial. And in the perspective of our own century, these are notions with a sobering immediacy. The Christian must say, 'not without the Jewish victims of the death-camps'—not knowing what imaginable future would find us a common language with them. But it is more important to look unknowingly to such a future than to devise hasty Christian theologies of (definitions of?) the Jewish experience in this century, and to recognize that the Church remains incomplete and in some ways deprived of a fully truthful language for God so long as this wound is open.

That is a matter needing constantly more thought and prayer; but it is not wholly immaterial to what we should say about racism, power, and faith. We have seen a picture of the Church in its beginnings as a community challenging both externally and internally the idea of persons being 'told who they are' by the possessors of a certain kinds of status. We are all to find who we are in the light of God in Jesus, and that finding *is* the process of living in a community struggling to discover means of mutual empowering and affirming, in the conviction that we shall not live or flourish if we consider any person or group dispensable, or merely functional for our own self-definition. And behind the life of such a community stands the event—and the *power*—by which it lives. To understand the Church, we must look at what generates it.

(*b*) Christian Scripture (which includes Jewish Scripture and is conditioned by it) answers the question of what God it is that Christians worship by relating the stories of communities: this is what a human group that believes itself to be brought into being by God looks like: from this group, you may learn what 'God' means, in its behaviour, its hymns and myths, laws and chronicles, in its social conflicts and resolutions. Above all, you may learn what 'God' means in the ministry and execution of Jesus, and in the re-creation of a faithful community in his name at Easter; you may learn God in this breakage and healing in the story of the community of God's people, 'the tribes of Yahweh',[10] as it becomes the beginning of a community for all nations.

The point is that the pattern of the Christian story shows a God who lets himself be spoken of—defined—in terms of the relation between him and creatures, in terms of the human history he sets in motion and shapes. He chooses to be the God of Israel and of Jesus Christ, chooses not to exist without his creation: he does not merely establish an order other than himself, but engages with it in such a way that we do not and cannot speak of him only as a remote cause, but must 'define' him in and through the lives that struggle to respond to his pressure and presence. Humanity is defined by him; but, for us, God is defined by humanity also—never completely or adequately, because the relation is always a restless and growing one. Yet the most basic point of reference for the Christian believer, which justifies and establishes this possibility and regulates what *kind* of humanity it is that 'carries' the definition of God, is the crucified and glorified human identity of Jesus. Whatever else is to be said, whatever further shifts and developments our language about God undergoes, this at least remains: God is not to be spoken of without humanity, but that humanity is centred not upon a generalized definition of the human, but on Jesus Christ.

In other words, the relations that exist *within* the Church, of mutual gift and reciprocal definition, are founded upon the fact that the Christian God reveals himself, becomes utterable, in a mortal human history. God, so to speak, risks himself in the form of vulnerable humanity—because a particular human life, Jesus, is given to him freely to be a sign and a word. The pattern of mutual definition, the *admirabile commercium* of classical theology, is the ground of the Church's speech and action, so that within its life it seeks to renounce just that kind of unilateral and invulnerable power that God renounces in the history he shares with us as the God of Israel and as Christ. God does not impose his definition and meaning by clear and absolute words of relevation, but perfects his speech to us in and through the contingencies of Israel's and Jesus's

---

[10] The title of Norman Gottwald's important study of the meaning of God for ancient Israel in terms of the pattern of their social life (London, 1979).

history. While in retrospect we may see a logic, even a necessity, in the whole story, it is at each *particular* point a matter of human liberty and risk.

These theological refinements may seem to be a long way from our starting-point; but they may provide a firm basis for a theological critique of racism to the extent that they spell out the nature of Christianity's attitude to power. We are not talking about a repudiation of the whole notion of power, as a hasty reading of the tradition might suggest, but about how the creative and transfiguring power of God actually is seen in our world. God's power 'tells us who we are' only in the risk and reciprocity of God's life with us in Christ, as God displays his identity in the terms of human freedom and human vulnerability. That is the power by which the whole world is given newness of life, humanity itself is given new definition. And because it is *that* kind of power, refusing to functionalize and enslave what it works with, the process of preaching a transfiguring gospel must take place in a community that resists the idea that one human group can ever have licence to define another in terms of its own needs or goals or fantasies. All must be free to find that ultimate self-definition in the encounter with a God who does not use us as tools for his gratification but shares a world of risk and contingency with us to bring us to' our fullest liberty in relation with him and each other.

We have seen that this cannot be without conflict and rupture, or without cost to those who claim the power of definition without noticing that this is what they are doing (and yes; it must be said again that the very enterprise of writing as a white academic about racism runs this risk). The Church has been slow to see how and where it is itself trapped in 'telling people who they are'; it is gradually getting used at least to the *idea* that its institution and decision-makers must learn a new tentativeness in listening to those they have assumed they understood—those they have assumed were 'contained' in the categories they work with. But the concrete redefinition of power—as enabling the stranger to be heard, deciding that the stranger has a gift and a challenge that can change you—limps very slowly, in the Church's listening to the voice of women and homosexuals·as much as blacks. We are still desperately ill equipped to do what, with daily increasing urgency, presses to be done: to offer our world an effective, a converting, judgement upon a whole culture of exploitative control—the human crisis mentioned earlier in this paper. And we are ill equipped partly because we have so imperfectly heard this judgement as it is passed upon *us* as a Church. What a Church genuinely converted in this respect *can* offer, in judgement and in promise, to the world is something we can, thank God, glimpse in the effect of the lives of those who, like Trevor Huddleston, have responded with integrity to what the Christian gospel has to say about true and false power, who have so let God, and God alone, 'tell them who they are' in Christ that they are free to free others for that encounter. Such lives show us something of what it might be to grow *together* in discovery and definition 'Till the Judgement morning'.

The Religious Understanding of Human Rights and Racism

JOHN BOWKER

THIS paper was originally presented, as a basis for discussion, to a United Nations working party convened by Trevor Huddleston. The purpose of that gathering was to produce a statement on religions and apartheid, with particular reference to human rights and racism. The paper is offered to him now, in this volume, in gratitude for his unwavering guidance and inspiration, from the moment when *Naught for Your Comfort* alerted many of us for the first time to the real meaning in effect of apartheid, down to the present day.

The paper moves through three stages. First, it points out that it is not immediately obvious that religions are allies in contesting apartheid or discrimination, because there is much in their histories which has moved in comparable directions. In the first part of this paper, we will look, very quickly, at some examples of what that means.

Secondly, religion has raised a countervailing protest against its own history, out of its own principles and resources; and it has also learned (though often reluctantly) to accept the protest of outsiders. So the question will be asked whether the many religious protests and the history of its moral struggle form a better basis for arriving at a definition of human rights; again it is by no means obvious that they do so, because religions simply do not agree on what it means to be human.

Thirdly and finally, we have to ask, what *can* religions,

given this background, contribute to an understanding of human rights and the contest against racism?

To begin with the first of these warning notes, there is a danger that we might merely point out the obvious. If you assemble representatives of world religions and ask if they are opposed to racism and to apartheid, the answer is going to be, Yes. It is somewhat like assembling a benediction of bishops and asking them if they are against sin. Obviously they are—or at least, they have to say that they are. So for a group to endorse the obvious—that religions are opposed to racism and to apartheid—seems superfluous. It is like the famous remark attributed to Carlyle, who, when Margaret Fuller proclaimed with a romantic gesture, 'I accept the universe', commented, 'By God, she'd better'.

And yet, of course, it is *not* so obvious that religions would automatically oppose at least *some* of those forms of categorization and discrimination which underlie racism, since they have supported and justified actions and institutions in their own histories which have led to the denial of opportunities and freedoms to particular people on the basis of religious categories. After all, apartheid had an original attempted justification in biblical exegesis, although that has now been firmly and unequivocally repudiated, not only by Christians in general, but by the World Alliance of Reformed Churches.

Nevertheless, the history of religions does not make it obviously necessary that religions would be natural allies in any contest against apartheid.

That may seem strange at first sight, particularly for those who have seen the film on Gandhi, or who in any case know the story of his life, and remember his early protest against discrimination in South Africa; or when one considers the long, deep, and often sacrificial protest against the fact of apartheid among, not only Christians, but members of other religions, including the indigenous traditions of the Africans.

Yet the other fact remains, that religions, including Hinduism (since it has just been mentioned) and certainly including Christianity, have supported, and sometimes created, social, political, economic, educational, and ecclesiastical realities and institutions which deny individuals even a limited opportunity to dispose of their lives with at least *something* like the same freedom as others in the same society. Even more to the point (which is the key to apartheid), religions have categorized people, not only sometimes by race, but also by sex, by conformity, by birth; and they have categorized them in such a way that people in those categories are deprived of particular opportunities which others enjoy.

Even without those obstacles, the freedom to dispose of ourselves as we will is limited: we are limited by time (we cannot live several lives at once); we are limited by genetic endowment (which is *not* a racist comment: this is a much more elementary observation, that we have, for example, arms instead of wings or fins, and that we are limited from flying as freely as birds, or swimming as superbly as fish); we are limited also by competition: this planet is tinier than even the merest twinkle in the eye of the entire universe, and yet it is evidently far too large for us to cope with: it is too large in the sense that we have not yet found, nor even begun to find, how to share its resources among ourselves; and that inequality severely limits what seven-eighths of the population of this planet can do.

So we are already restricted in what we can do with the opportunity of our lives. Yet on top of those natural limitations, religions impose more. Indeed, because religions are organized to ensure the transmission of traditions (traditions which contain saving or enlightening truth) from one generation to another, they frequently add a further dead weight to the inertia which enables one group to continue, through centuries, to exploit another. In fact Nietzsche used to argue that bishops *are*, in a paradoxical way, in favour of sin, because it gives them a handle and a control over believers: ' "Sins" are indispensable to every society organized on an ecclesiastical basis; they are the only reliable weapons of power; the priest lives upon sins; it is necessary to him that there be "sinning".'

So religions, at least in the past, have almost always operated strong systems of control, transmission, and boundary maintenance—not least in the sense of 'who is in and who is out'—while at the same time pointing to universal concepts, such as the single *umma* of all humans in Islam, or the universal *atman* in Hinduism, or Paul's proclamation that there is 'neither Jew nor Greek, neither bond nor free, neither male nor female, for you are all one in Christ Jesus'.

But to belong to such universals of faith, or to realize such universals of existence, one has to make an active movement of assent; so the Church could still say, *extra ecclesiam nulla salus est* (outside the Church there is no salvation); Hinduism could still elaborate a complex and rigid form of the caste system; and Islam could still divide the world into *dar ulIslam* and *dar ulHarb*—simply to stay with those examples.

Religions are therefore exceptionally vulnerable to a version of the double-standards argument. In its political form, that argument claims that protesters against apartheid or racism would be a great deal more convincing if they generated a comparable energy against the oppression operated, with evident impunity, by the Soviet Union: why stop playing cricket with the South Africans, when you go on playing the Olympic games with the Russians, and in Moscow?

Against religions the double-standards argument is rather more subtle: it is the argument that religions have created and maintained exactly those designations of order, status, duty, and role which they are now condemning, *mutatis mutandis*, in apartheid. So, the defender of apartheid (of separate development) might argue, 'what you, in your own histories, have discovered, that the alternative to chaos is a well and strongly ordered arrangement of society, is what we are doing here, in apartheid; and what you, in world religions, should be doing, is to bring your experience of highly ordered societies to help, not hinder, separate development'.

That may not seem to be a convincing argument. But if religions are to respond to racism and to apartheid, they need to be aware of the internal logic which has led them in comparable, or at least apparently comparable, directions. Any attempt to organize an effective religious and inter-religious protest against racism or apartheid lacks reality, if it does not *first* come to terms (and deeply penitent terms) with its own failures. But then, precisely because religions *have* come to that clearer understanding of the intolerable and the evil in their own case—and in so far as they have taken action against it—their protest has much greater authority.

What, then, does it mean to suggest that religions have

been led, at times, in comparable directions? Let me give some brief and familiar examples. Gandhi, and his protests against injustice and discrimination in South Africa, has already been mentioned. He had equally to protest against the effects of the caste system in India, promoting the untouchables to Harijans (Children of God) and conducting one of his 'fasts unto death' in 1932 to stop Dr Ambedkar, the leader of the Depressed Classes, from gaining a separate electorate for the untouchables on the ground that they were as much a separate minority from the Hindus as were the Muslims—they were that far removed, in his view, from Hindu society and religion. Gandhi insisted that they must be integrated and literally embraced, so he opposed the separate electorate—and paid a high price for doing so: under the Poona Pact, the number of seats for Ambedkar's constituency was increased from 71 to 148. Yet even so, Ambedkar continued to observe. 'To ask people to give up caste is to ask them to go contrary to their fundamental religious notions'; and Dr Srinivas, who argued powerfully that the British insistence on caste equality was a disingenuous technique of dividing Hindus in order to rule them, maintained, 'if and when caste disappears, Hinduism will also disappear'.

It is certainly possible for Hindus to follow Gandhi in believing that the elaboration of the caste system (which has restricted the opportunities for many individuals and groups to dispose of their lives as they will) was an aberration, a betrayal of the original vision of the Vedas. When making *Worlds of Faith* (a survey of what the major religions mean to their believers in Britain today), I interviewed many Hindus, and one of them put it even more strongly: 'The reason for this caste system has nothing to do with religion. It's a social development: wherever you find society you find division of labour. But now the caste system has become a real menace: it has stopped all growth, all improvement, you see.'

That argument is an example, in the case of Hinduism, of an internal moral struggle, in which it is certainly possible to see the extreme elaboration of the much simpler caste system into a rigid system of classification and discrimination as a conceptual episode, which has its own history, and which may have its own intelligible origin, and also its decline and fall *without* the destruction of Hinduism. The caste system is certainly less strong now in urban areas of India, and clearly much less strong in Britain—except where marriage is concerned. Inter-caste marriage is for most Hindus still something to be avoided if possible. This is true even of Sikhs, who are supposed to have abolished the caste system. One of the most often-quoted sayings of Guru Nanak is: 'There is neither Hindu nor Muslim, so whose path do I follow? I shall follow God's path. God is neither Hindu nor Muslim, and the path which I follow is God's.' Yet Sikhs have maintained their own version of the caste system, although many of them recognize the hypocrisy of it, as a Sikh wife told me:

That is the essence of Guru Nanak's teaching, that there is no caste system, although we do have it. That's a sort of hypocrisy, really: there is no caste system; and if they are true Sikhs, there should be no caste system. But there is: there's the Jats, the Khans, there's so many. When it comes to marriage, you marry inside your caste.

And if we are talking of marriage, what are we to make of that other example of religion strongly determining, on the basis of classification, what a person may or may not do with her life, and that is the determination by men of what women may and may not do?

> Mama, what is a feminist?
> A feminist, my daughter,
> is one who cares or dares
> to take in charge her own affairs
> when men don't think she oughter.

Of course we are all familiar with the argument that women themselves *prefer* this attributed status, because it protects the family, it secures their own position, it makes them more important than men—the wife as 'queen of the home', 'light of the household', 'equal but different', as the rose is equal to the lily, but nevertheless different.

Suppose we accept that all those arguments are correct—and they certainly have been put forward with great vigour not only by men, but by women. Nevertheless this attributed status restricts women to certain possibilities in their lives by definition—a definition, not now of race, but of sex. This attribution virtually *all* religions have maintained, and some still do. The title of the protest by William Thompson in 1825 makes the point exactly: *The Appeal of One Half [of] the Human Race, Women, against the Pretensions of the Other Half, Men, to Retain them in Political, and thence in Civil and Domestic Slavery.* And consider how relevant one of his arguments still is to what we are considering: 'Women expect no removal of *natural* bars to their success. All they ask is, that to these natural bars in the way of their pursuit of equal happiness with men, no additional bars, no *factitious* restraints, shall be super-added.'

This is not an attempt to divert the discussion into the issue of women's rights. I am simply pointing out that many of the arguments advanced by religious believers to justify this are close to arguments used to justify apartheid, particularly the arguments that they are really better off under this system, that it is in their own best interest, and that this is what they really prefer. Some years ago a photo appeared in *South African Panorama*, of African women hoeing vegetables; and the caption read: 'The women tend the vegetable gardens, not only because their menfolk are away working in nearby Pinetown and Durban, but also because it is an added form of exercise.'

The wit of man (and it usually *is* man in such cases, and not woman) can usually find a justification for anything. A world that can justify sending its leaders to the most exclusive and expensive holiday island, in order to come to the conclusion that it will do nothing of any real substance to implement the Brandt Report, is capable of justifying anything. Consider slavery, which is by no means eliminated yet, and which religions have both tolerated and maintained.

It is well known that early Christians brought to existing institutions the imperative of love (of *agape*) and thus changed, at least potentially for the better, the nature of those relations, between husband and wife, children and parents, owners and slaves. But they did not change the institution of slavery, at least for many centuries. And when the change did come, it was ferociously resisted within the religious domain, and with (sometimes) specifically religious arguments.

The same kind of dilemma is true in Islam. One of the points repeatedly and rightly made about Islam is that it changed and improved the condition of slaves, as it did also that of women. Can the process of change and improvement continue? Since the Qur'ān is *the* uncorrupted record of the revelation from God, and since also it is illustrated in the *sunna* of the prophet, of whom Sayyeda 'A'isha said, 'His character was the Qur'ān', what is stated in the Qur'ān and Muslim tradition is not open to change. It is open, obviously, to exegesis and to application; but nothing can conceivably abrogate the Qur'ān; and why *should* the Qur'ān be abrogated, when it *is* the Word of God, making clear the nature of the society which he wills? Consequently, any attempt to introduce an abstract charter of 'human rights' or 'rights for women', or for that matter the abolition of slavery, will have to be subordinate to the Qur'ān, and not the other way round. Yet Muslims certainly recognize the fact of contingency (the fact that the Qur'ān is *always* contingently related to the circumstances of *each* prophet), and that consequently its application must itself recognize the reality of our own contingency. It therefore *is* possible for Muslims both to see the legitimacy of polygamy or of slavery, and to recognize its lapse in the particular circumstances in which they live.

Even without the sanction of revelation, the abolition of slavery was no easy task. Coming back to Christianity, so monumental was the opposition to change that John Wesley, in the last letter he wrote, on the day before he died, felt that Wilberforce would be well nigh destroyed if he went on. He wrote to Wilberforce:

My Dear Sir, unless the Divine Power has raised you up to be as Athanasius, *contra mundum*, I see not how you can go through your glorious enterprise in opposing that execrable villainy which is the scandal of religion, of England, and of human nature. Unless God has raised you up for this very thing, you will be worn out by the opposition of men and devils; but *if God be for you, who can be against you?* Are all of them together stronger than God? O, *be not weary in well-doing.* Go on, in the name of God and in the power of his might, until even American slavery, the vilest that ever saw the sun, shall vanish away before it.

Reading this morning a tract wrote by a poor African, I was particularly struck by the circumstance that a man who has a black skin, being wronged or outraged by a white man, can have no redress; it being a *law* in our colonies that the *oath* of a black against white goes for nothing. What villainy is this!

That he who has guided you from your youth up may continue to strengthen you in this and in all things is the prayer of, Dear Sir, Your affectionate Servant, John Wesley.

So if religions are to oppose racism or respond to apartheid, they need first to realize how much there is in their own history which has led in comparable directions: 'There is no social evil, no form of injustice, whether of the feudal or the capitalist order, which has not been sanctified in some way or another by religious sentiment and thereby rendered more impervious to change.'

Those words were written, not by Marx nor by a paid-up member of the rationalist society, but by a Christian philosopher much concerned with the social implications of religion, Reinhold Niebuhr—of whom William Temple once observed, 'He is the troubler of my peace.'

And that *is* the critical point: that phrase 'troubler of my peace' picks up the note of prophetic protest which religions also generate. Think of the names already mentioned: Gandhi, Guru Nanak, the prophet Muhammad, Wesley, Wilberforce. When individuals or groups who know their truth as a matter of experience and conviction find in the practice of a religion a contradiction of that truth and experience—or, indeed, a contradiction of the very demands which lie within the religion in question itself—then religions generate the protest against their own failure. It is out of that moral struggle that people have learnt, through pain and suffering, to recognize more clearly what is wrong.

Can we then move on from the history of religions, which is necessarily conservative (conserving the transmission of those saving truths which have given life and light to countless generations), to find a common ground of human rights within the prophetic protests which each religion evokes?

Superficially, yes: it would not be difficult to construct an anthology of texts which give absolute value to human freedom and dignity. That is exactly what UNESCO attempted, fifteen years ago, in a book entitled *The Birthright of Man*. Its opening words are:

To mark the 20th anniversary of the Universal Declaration of Human Rights, the General Conference of UNESCO suggested the idea of publishing a collection of quotations, drawn from a wide variety of traditions and periods, which, with their profound concordance enhanced by the diversity of their origins, would illustrate how human beings everywhere, throughout the ages and all over the world, have asserted and claimed the birthright of man.

Yet even here, *festina lente* (hasten slowly). It is unsafe to move directly from the realm of rhetoric to the arena of action because religions do not agree on what *is* the natural nature of men and women. Each religion carries its own implicit anthropology—that is to say, its own understanding of what belongs to this strange architecture of atoms constituting the human form and being; and each religion therefore carries its own understanding also of what this aggregation of energy is capable of being and becoming. To give a simple illustration: some years ago, a documentary was shown on British television of a return visit to the so-called 'death railway' constructed by prisoners of war under the supervision of Japanese guards. Part of the line has remained open, and at the end of the line there is now a flourishing plantation carved out of the jungle—a plantation which obviously could not have been brought into existence but for the railway. The interviewer asked the owner whether he had any uneasy feelings about his own prosperity having been built on so many deaths. He replied that of course he was sorry that it had happened, but that life comes and goes—and anyway, he asked (turning on the interviewer), why do you put such a value on the individual appearance on this earth?

Few things could summarize more graphically the difference between the anthropologies which occur in different religions. The apparent indifference to death which Americans encountered in the kamikaze pilots and later in Vietnamese guerrillas, and more recently among Shiite Muslims, not only took them by surprise, but made a nonsense of many of their military and political judgements. Each of those actions looks superficially the same: but the *reasons* for those actions within the three respective anthropologies are utterly different.

To take the Japanese case: there existed a distinctive sense of the close connection between the spirits of the dead and the soil of Japan and between the living and the spirit of their ancestors, as Kunio Yanagida has summarized:

We do not know how old this belief in the ancestral spirit remaining on this land of ours to protect their posterity and make them prosper may be. But it is important to note that the cosmopolitan idea of Buddhism, which preached that the departed soul would leave this land to go to some faraway place, for it did not belong within any national boundary, was very strange to the Japanese people. Surrounded by nations who believe the other world to be far away and cut off from them, and in spite of long years of Buddhist influence, the Japanese alone retained their belief in the closeness and accessibility of the departed spirits of their ancestors.

Those beliefs created a powerful justification for actions and attitudes in war which to other belief-systems seemed incomprehensible, or worse.

When the International Military Tribunal was set up in Japan in 1946, it classified war crimes in three categories: crimes against peace, conventional war crimes, and crimes against humanity. Crimes against humanity seemed self-evidently to be crimes of atrocity; yet the actual word 'humanity', as in 'human rights', begs the very question at issue: an atrocity in one anthropology is not necessarily so in another; and of the 1,068 prisoners who were executed (or who died in prison), it is clear that the majority remained committed to the view that their actions in the war were justified. 701 of those who died as war criminals left some kind of personal statement. The statements were collected and published under the title *Seiki no Isho*. An analysis of the statements showed that 87.4 per cent of those condemned refused to accept any kind of guilt, except that they had failed the Emperor and their fellow-countrymen (which was indeed Hideki Tojo's own attitude: 'As a man responsible for the waging of the war, I deeply regret that the war ended with our defeat. I deeply regret what I have done and apologize to the Emperor and to my countrymen'). Of those who refused to accept guilt, 30 per cent specifically expressed a belief that their spirits would return to protect their families and their fatherland, and for that reason they were able to approach their own death undisturbed.

I am not making any value judgement here, simply pointing

out that religions do not easily lend themselves to concrete definitions of human rights, because their sense of what constitutes the human differs. If, for example, we are constituted in such a way that our *jiva* (*atman* in its temporal projection and attachment) may be reborn as many as 84,000,000 times, there is clearly nothing like the same urgency to act now, within this brief space of 'three score years and ten'. In fact, exactly the reverse: our present circumstance is the manifestation of *karma* as consequence. *Karma* is not particularly reward or punishment, it is simply the appropriate consequence of what we have done in previous lives, for good or for ill; and in this Buddhists agree even though they reject very strongly the belief that there *is* such a reality as *atman* or *jiva* being reborn. ' The body by its nature', as Govinda has put it of Buddhism, 'is just materialised *karma*, the consciousness of past moments of existence made visible.' In the case of Hinduism, the caste system simply formalizes the levels of consequence, and it makes it much simpler for individuals to know exactly how to act and how to behave: they will know, within the boundary of caste, what the *dharma* (the right and proper thing to do) is, so that any future birth will manifest the good consequence of that conformity; and in that way it can be argued, as Vivekananda and many others have argued, that 'caste is a natural order'. Note the words (in those last two quotations) 'nature' and 'natural': there is an appeal to human *nature*. But the Buddhist and the Hindu, while agreeing on *karma/kamma* as consequence, nevertheless *dis*agree on identifying the nature of the subject of that consequence— *atman* in Hinduism, *anatta* (no-self or soul) in Buddhism.

Yet in either case, the person understood as a manifestation of karmic consequence is very different from the 'men are born and remain free and equal in rights' of the French Revolution. But that is precisely the point to seize hold of: for the men and citizens of the French Revolution are themselves the product of a particular history, and the producers of another; and the most immediate history they helped to produce was one of even greater assurance: 'We hold these truths to be self-evident, that all men are created equal, that they are endowed by their Creator with certain inalienable Rights, that among these are Life, Liberty, and the pursuit of Happiness.'

But they are not self-evident: they are a consequence of a particular history *which is still continuing*. And that is the point where religions can (and in my view *must*) have something of real substance to contribute, and not a mere anthology of rhetorical adornment. The concept of a person, and of what it means to be human, and of what it is that racism denies, is constantly on the move. Consider even the title of the UNESCO book: who now would dare to call such a book 'The Birthright of *Man*'? Where are the women and children? Yes, of course, 'man' was and is generic. But surely now we would have a greater sensitivity. This change has been wrought in a mere fifteen years. The word person/persona has gone through even longer and equally revolutionary changes. It was taken to come from the verb *persono*, 'I sound through', because the original meaning of persona was a mask, especially used on the stage by actors to represent different parts in a play; and it was through these masks (or rather, through large openings in these masks) that the actors spoke. From there, the word, not surprisingly, came to mean, not just the mask worn by the actor, but the part he was thereby playing; and hence persona came to mean the part that anybody plays in the world. In Cicero, it is virtually the career one chooses, as opposed to the circumstances one inherits by birth or by accident.

Regal powers and military commands, nobility of birth and political office, wealth and influence, and their opposites, depend upon chance and are, therefore, controlled by circumstances. But what *personam* we ourselves may choose to sustain is decided by our own free choice. And so some turn to philosophy, others to the civil law, and still others to oratory.

All that talk of play-acting, pretence, acting out parts, is a long way from the person possessed of rights of the French Revolution and the Declaration of Independence. How did this revolution in the understanding of what a person means come about? Obviously, it has a history: and the point is that that history is continuing, and religions ought to have a part to play in defining the next stage of that history. Looking back, we can see (and learn from) the stages of that history in creating and changing the concept of what it means to be human, to be a person. One was Roman law itself, which transformed the person from an actor on a stage to a participant in an ordered society. The second revolution was the long debate about Christology and the Trinity in the early Christian centuries, because it had to be understood how Jesus could be two natures in one *Person*; and how God could be three *Persons* in one Godhead. A third gain was to clarify how the soul is conferred by God on individuals as the means of their identity and persistence, the continuing subject of their own experience and agent of their own actions, and thus the form of the body.

So the Ciceronian person has the right to a range of choices (if the state and the status of birth so dispose): the Christian person has status because his or her identity as self or soul is directly created by God and is inviolable. If you then put the two together, the rights of the person are constituted by that identity, whether the State likes it or not. And that combination proves to be explosive.

Obviously, the history was nothing like as crude or simple as that, but Renaissance man did become possessed of his own person in a sense that a feudal tenant did not; and states were constituted (or rather, some believed that they *should* be constituted) by free agents giving themselves to the service and support of others—much as Pétain said, when he signed the armistice with the Germans in 1940, 'Je fais le don de ma personne à la France' (I am making the gift of my person to France). Of course, there were other political theories, and other views of the corporate State. But there now broke through at least the vision of the person possessed of rights as much as of obligations. It is a very disturbing sense of person, because it confers on every individual an autonomy which he or she may well use to turn around and destroy the very process which has enabled him or her to be precisely that person. We grow into the possession of our own selves—which is actually what every person has to do in order to become an independent adult. As the saying has it: there is nothing wrong with teenagers that a good argument won't make worse. And there is another saying of the same kind: if you think sometimes, as a parent, that your children are losing their faith, don't forget that it may be *your* faith they are losing, while they find their own.

To the operators and controllers of any system, whether political *or* religious, such independence is an almost unbearable thought. And it is they, whether in the Kremlin or in Pretoria, who try to *reverse* the history of the word 'person' and turn individuals back into the old persona, the mask, the hollow face, through which they, the controllers of thought, can speak.

Certainly there have been more than three revolutions in the concept of 'person'—the psychoanalytic would be a fourth; the discoveries of genetic research are constituting a fifth which will be of great importance in the protest against racism, because the implications of much of that research emphasize the unity of the human subspecies at the same time as it manifests important adaptive diversity. In any case, in addition to the transformations in *Western* history, there have been Eastern histories as well, diverging and changing with equal drama. The point is that the concept of a person is not *fixed*, it is *achieved*. And what is required of religions now is that they contribute to that coalition of understanding which will constitute the next stage of the achievement.

What then will be lost if religions refuse this challenge—if they rest, defensively, in their own history (as they are often tempted to do), and believe that 'the human' is already defined exhaustively in their own system? What will be lost will be the adequacy of the continuing definition of the human, and therefore ultimately what will be lost will be any adequate defence of humanity.

So, to turn the question the other way round, what do religions in particular contribute to the next sense of being human? What *can* they contribute collectively, given the extreme diversity of their anthropologies? There is, I think, one point on which (not despite, but because of, the diversity of their understanding of human nature) they must insist: and that is the affirmation and acquisition of responsibility. They may have many other things to say—either separately, or in agreement—but on this they must insist *together*, because, in all their diversity, it is *this* which all religions maintain and defend; that to be human is to accept and acquire responsibility. No matter how different (and in fact radically incompatible) are their descriptions of what it is to be human (which, as I keep emphasizing, makes it a very diverse adjective when attached to the word 'rights'), they do agree that what constitutes the human as opposed to—say—the sand or the snow is the acquisition of one's own life as a matter of one's own responsibility; and therefore to be human is necessarily to be accountable. As Muslims put it succinctly, quoting the Qur'ān over a dying person, 'To God we belong, and to Him we return.'

None of this is to deny that as humans we are constructed within tight boundaries and constraints. We are limited by time, by space, by competition, by genetic programmes. But we are *not* so limited as other organizations of energy; and indeed one of the great insights of modern biology is that the more complex the genetic programmes are, and the more elaborate the hierarchies of organic construction become, the *greater* the degree of freedom for the resulting animal. Lewis Thomas makes the point:

The solitary wasp, Sphex, nearing her time of eggs, travels aloft with a single theory about caterpillars. She is, in fact, a winged receptor for caterpillars. Finding one to match the hypothesis, she swoops, pins it, paralyses it, carries it off and descends to deposit it precisely in front of the door of the round burrow (which, obsessed by a different version of the same theory, she had prepared beforehand). She drops the beast, enters the burrow, inspects the interior for last-minute irregularities, then comes out to pull it in for egg-laying. It has the orderly step-wise look of a well-thought-out business. But if, while she's inside inspecting, you move the caterpillar a short distance, she has a less sensible second thought about the matter. She emerges, searches for a moment, finds it, drags it back to the original spot, drops it again, and runs inside to check the burrow again. If you move the caterpillar again, she will repeat the programme, and you can keep her totally preoccupied for as long as you have the patience and the heart for it. It is a compulsive, essentially neurotic kind of behaviour, as mindless as an Ionesco character, for the wasp cannot imagine any other way of doing the thing.

But we can: constructed from far more complex and

elaborate genetic programmes, we can not only imagine but also act on the basis of our imaginations. This is the point at which the religious understanding of human rights and of what it means to be human begins. There may be many other, and more specific, things which they wish to say, but, fundamentally, all religions accept and emphasize the fact that we are born and constructed within extremely tight boundaries of constraint which are not chosen: they are a fact of life or, more accurately, of birth. Religions may talk about it in very different and totally incompatible terms of, for example, original sin, or *karma*, or *qadr*, or *berith*. But in those different ways they are saying that we are *not* born wholly free and independent of what has gone before us, and that that happens to be the way the cookie of creation crumbles.

Far from resting at that point, however, as do racist politics and interpretations, as though that is the end of the matter, religions see it as the beginning—and the opportunity—of all that it means to be human. For what they also say anticipates a great insight of cybernetics, that where a constraint exists, advantage can usually be taken of it. In other words, the more clearly you know and understand the complex limitations which circumscribe your possible activity, the more you are set free for actual achievement. It is an artificial and brutal contradiction of nature to condemn any human to the mere programmes of its possibility. Indeed, such a thought should be a complete self-contradiction. The point is this: if you wish to set foot on the moon, you cannot do so by standing in a field and flapping your arms 'in mere despair of wings'; but when you understand the constraints which stop you (such things as pressure, gravity, oxygen) and act on the basis of that understanding, you are set free to build a rocket and eventually to set foot on the moon.

Religions say exactly the same: the more you understand and accept the reality of the conditions which alone allow you to be alive, the more you are set free (or should be set free) for the exploration of human possibility. In other words, born into a circumstance without choice, you begin, as you grow up, to acquire your self; and that means, religiously, that you accept the fact that you are responsible for what you set forward (or fail to set forward) in your own life; and it means accepting also that you are accountable: 'In as much as you have done it [or failed to do it] to the least one of these, you have done it [or failed to do it] to me.'

There is no *compulsion* to live in this way. That is why it is a specifically *religious* contribution to the definition of what it means to be human, and therefore of human rights. Others *may* live in this way—and they often do: non-religious, anti-religious, secularist, and humanist individuals frequently live in this character of responsibility, and with a serious sense of their own accountability, and they do so, frequently, in more heroic and consistent ways than believers. Nevertheless, the fact remains that religious belivers *must* live in this way, or fall into exactly that condemnation of hypocrisy, contradiction, and betrayal which all religions insist is culpable, often reinforcing the point with terrifying descriptions of its consequence in hell-fire and torment.

I am not suggesting that we should revive the Buddhist, Hindu, Christian, or any other imagination of hell-fire as a literal punishment with which to threaten people. Spiritual terrorization contradicts precisely this vital insight about the human acquisition of its own responsibility (which is, incidentally, much more fundamental to religions and very much earlier in their history than any imaginations of hell-fire, or for that matter of heaven). If you terrorize individuals or control them into the conformity of a Sphex wasp performing the behaviours that you prescribe for them, you destroy precisely that process of growth—of growing into a willingness to accept and assume responsibility—which is the religious mark of being human.

But exactly the reverse is also true: if you must not terrorize people into the exercise of responsibility, equally, you must not destroy the possibility of their being *able* to exercise it for themselves. It is here that the specific issues of human rights (or, really, of the right to be human in a religious way) come flooding in. This is why there can be, and has to be, a religious protest against poverty, against racism, against the male determination of what women may or may not do, against Leninist imperialism, against Coca Cola imperialism, against apartheid, against any contradiction of that basic religious insight that you cannot ask people to acquire and accept responsibility for the disposition of their own lives (as religions say they must) if you put them or control them in circumstances where there is no space and no way in which to be responsible.

None of this is to argue against the *option* to live in circumstances which others could not endure: many Hindu, Muslim, Sikh wives and mothers look at marriage, sex, and the family in the West, and they do not like what they see. They therefore opt for their traditional ways. The only issue of human rights is whether it is genuinely an option, a free donation (so far as that can ever be the case) of their person in that way rather than another. Sometimes it will be, sometimes it will not.

But racism defines itself as far beyond that boundary, because those on the receiving end of racist abuse (by which I mean not just verbal or physical attack, but jobs, pay, housing, all the rest of it) have no option. They can make no choice about it. It is this which makes apartheid inhumane—a contradiction of any and every notion of human rights and of humanity.

This requirement of responsibility is universal. It is laid on us by each religious tradition. On that foundation, we can then go on to draw from the wisdom of each tradition those insights which have a bearing on apartheid.

Which brings us full circle: do we really *need* to argue for the foundation of a religious understanding of what it means to be human in this way? It would be a happier world if it were not so necessary. It is indeed so obvious that it *should* scarcely need saying. But clearly the fact is, in South Africa and Namibia, that it is not obvious to everyone. Perhaps this whole argument may seem academic and useless. There is a cartoon which makes the point: two unemployed young people are standing in a derelict inner-city wasteland, and one says to the other 'Charlie—are you a rationally autonomous person whose life is self-directed in the light of what reason determines?'

To conclude, therefore, let me refer to a handwritten note which Max Scheler added to the manuscript of one of his greatest works, *Der Formalismus in der Ethick* . . . Scheler, an outstanding moral philosopher, tried to establish persistent values at the foundation of ethical judgement, on the basis of a phenomenology of human relationships—and what could sound more remote and academic than that? Yet in the margin of his manuscript he wrote: 'Schleißlich ist Ethik einer verdammt blutige Sache . . .': 'At the end of the day, ethics is a damned bloody affair; and if it cannot give me directions on how I ought to be and to live now, in this social and historical context—well, what is it then?' And Scheler then added another note in the margin: 'the path from eternity, or from the *amor intellectualis sub specie quadam aeternitatis*, in which a glimmer of eternity becomes visible, "Today" and "Here" is immeasurably long. But it is precisely the task of philosophy to bridge, however indirectly, this gap.'

But in the end, it is not philosophy that can bridge this gap: it is life. Or rather, it is the particular lives of those who, in the acquisition of themselves as responsible and accountable, embrace the particularities of other lives, *sub specie quadam aeternitatis* (under a particular light of eternity, and not out of some temporal or mundane consideration which tries to work out what *I* can gain from it for myself).

There is no route to human rights via rhetoric: it is a bloody business—literally so, in prison cells in South Africa and on the streets of Soweto. Good will is not enough: good grief will take us further. As Richard Bentley put it, centuries ago, 'It was an excellent saying of Solon's who when he was asked what would rid the world of injuries replied, "if the bystanders would have the same resentment with those that suffer wrong".'

In that spirit, Jesse Jackson returned from South Africa with these words:

I hear the words of a song in Crossroads, South Africa, ringing out in my soul today. Those children in the pits of exploitation—no bathrooms, no running water, no right to vote, no political protection, no judicial regard—were there with nothing but their religion. They said that just because we are in the slums, the slums are not in us. We will rise above our circumstances.

They will rise even further if we will bear them up in hands that do not add to their injuries. In *all* religions prayer is entrusted to us as a means of love—an *effective* means of love. We will pray without ceasing. And we will act. God knows, as indeed he does know, white people have had their centuries of killing and beating and brutalizing black people. We cannot undo the past. But we can help to make the future. And if we are ever unsure what to do when we feel that resentment with those who suffer wrong, then we can always remember the single and simple advice of Helder Camara: 'If you choose the poor, you always choose rightly.'

We need to summon up the resources of all religions to make that choice. We must insist, as much to our leaders as to our local communities—and indeed, to ourselves—that we make that choice. We have to create that resentment of injury and that choice of the poor. The specific religious contribution to human rights is to define more adequately what it means to be human—the acquisition of our own responsibility and the acceptance that we *are* accountable; and the endeavour to ensure that possibility for all others. When Jefferson contemplated slavery, he once said: 'I tremble sometimes for my country, when I reflect that God is just.'

We have even more reason to tremble if we think that God is nothing.

Christology and Protest

DONALD M. MACKINNON

It is a very saddening feature of contemporary ecclesiastical controversy that discrimination is often sacrificed in the interests of a debased fanaticism. Thus the advocates of a continuing, formal orthodoxy are quick to accuse men and women of a more liberal outlook of bland compromise with prevailing secular attitudes, and those whom they accuse are driven to an impatient disregard of inherited perspectives, as if their confused obscurity was simply indicative of intellectual and spiritual poverty.

We are often oblivious of the fact that in the gospel tradition the question 'What think you of Christ?' is presented as posed not in the setting of a synod or council, but at Caesarea Philippi before the last journey to Jerusalem began, by the man who (again in the narrative) is represented as alone knowing that journey's outcome. Though Simon, son of John, is accounted blest because the Father has disclosed to him the secret beyond ratiocination (Matthew), the implications are more than he can bear, and he shows the sad limit of his comprehension by seeking to dissuade the Son of Man from his appointed way. The lesson is surely clear, and abides any defensible verdict on the historical foundation of the story. From Christ there issues a continually repeated question, and his Church is his authentic servant only so far as it allows that interrogation to continue. It is always easier to escape its remorseless probing: to take refuge in the security of a sharply defined orthodoxy, or to blur the riddling quality of its disturbing challenge by conformity to the standards of the age. 'Here we have no continuing city.' The sentence speaks not simply of the fact that Christianity has inescapably an other-worldly dimension, but of the fact that, in the place where the Church's confessions and strivings come to rest, that is, where the secret of Jesus Christ is made known, there is not the kind of security we naturally demand, but the insistence that we allow ourselves to be questioned again. 'Not as the world gives, give I unto you.' 'I have many things to say unto you: but you cannot bear them now.'

In the kinds of controversy in which Trevor Huddleston has been engaged, the problem of the use of force and violence (the two terms are of course not synonymous) has been repeatedly thrust on his attention, and it is indeed an issue on which the historical traditions of the Christian churches might be judged singularly unhelpful. In the situation that followed Constantine's conversion, the cautious words of Paul, addressed seemingly to Jewish Christians in Rome in the sixties of the first century AD, concerning the providential significance of the powers that be (in this case the Emperor Nero), received a new interpretation: Constantine's 'vision' and the supposedly congruous event of Helena's finding of the 'true Cross' came near imbuing imperial dignity with a numinous quality. Worse, as Whitehead, for instance, pointed out in the haunting Christological chapter of his opaque metaphysical masterpiece *Process and Reality*,[1] the Christian God was endowed imaginatively with the attributes of a human Caesar. The Galilean image, already for Whitehead obscured by thought of a remorseless lawgiver and an ontologically remote first mover, himself unmoved, is finally obscured by the rendering in supposed homage to God himself the likeness of a transcendent Caesar. The desert where Christ disdained at once the kingdoms of this world and their glory, and the sort of religious revivalism that would stun men and women into a morally uncomprehending acceptance of his claim (itself decisively changed in substance by the manner in which he would seek to impose it), is forgotten. For if Jesus emerged from that conflict as one who repudiated the road of earthly

---

[1] Cambridge, 1929.

power, he also emerged as one who was resolved (in obedience to his Father) to render himself completely vulnerable to the demands made on him by the very different men and women who would press on him for enlightenment, for healing, for judgement, for hope. If the built-in traditions of the churches have sought to insulate them from such testing and confused exposure, their aloofness often justified apologetically by reference to a devastatingly false other-worldliness on the one hand, and to the alleged congruity of the ways of God with those of Caesar on the other, that aloofness is very far from the vulnerability of the Nazarene.

Trevor Huddleston is certainly among those who in their life as well as in their words have been prepared to expose themselves to such experience, never shrinking from its contradictions. Further he can never be accused of indifference to the other-worldly dimension of Christian existence. A priest since 1937 and a member of the Community of the Resurrection since 1940, the seventy-fifth anniversary of his birth coincides with his jubilee in the priesthood: and although his life includes periods of service as bishop or archbishop in Tanzania, in Stepney, and in the area of the Indian Ocean, he has never sought to dissolve the bonds that since 1940 have bound him to the Community of the Resurrection. Again as an academic, I am impressed by the range and depth of his reading, only to remember that he obtained a good degree in modern history at Oxford in 1934. I mention these facts because they suggest that a deep and costly engagement with the issues of the societies in which Trevor Huddleston found himself ministering was not the expression of a reckless 'trendiness' but rather the inevitable consequence of a persistent religious fidelity. Moreover that fidelity, nurtured by a life of prayer, could itself only be sustained through that exposure to a whole number of often conflicting pressures. If in this essay I allow myself some free-ranging reflections on the ministry of Jesus, I do so confident that Trevor Huddleston would ask nothing more for himself than to constrain men and women to reflect on the 'author and finisher' of his faith and theirs. 'Oh, yet consider it again.' So Charles Gore, founder of the Community of the Resurrection, ended the short book on Jesus of Nazareth which he contributed nearly sixty years ago

to the Home University Library,[2] by issuing an imperative
that must be repeatedly obeyed across one's entire life-span,
and that not only in *theoria*, but in *praxis*.

There are various routes to the kind of aloofness that
debases the currency of one's understanding. But certainly
one of the most beguiling of these routes today is that which,
in a perfectly proper disdain for a febrile social activism, looks
back at some allegedly definitive embodiment of a sane religious
tradition which is thought menaced by an ill-considered
radicalism. The radical outlook moreover is judged tainted by
the values of secular humanism (sometimes quite inaccurately
identified with hedonistic utilitarianism), and seen as indifferent
to the claims of a more deeply religious sensibility. It is
dismissed as a shallow substitute for the more reverent, more
prudent attitude which traditional structures supposedly
safeguard and seek to perpetuate. Yet the sort of aloofness
from the present that such criticism encourages is itself
theologically sterile.

The most impressive contribution to Christology recently to
come to my notice is the essay contributed to the February
issue of the review *Encounter*[3] by the Jewish savant Professor
George Steiner. The article begins by reminding the reader
that any discussion of the issues of which it treats (broadly
speaking, the state of contemporary Western culture) must
recall, as the fundamental fact of this century, the Holocaust,
or Shoah, as Steiner prefers to call it. The word Auschwitz is
written large across the world we live in, and the article
(which ends with discussion of the work of the poet Celan)
probes the question of the *ultimate* ground of this elaborately
contrived rejection of the Jews of Europe, (rejection is the
wrong word—rubbishing surely a less inappropriate). 'Away
with them: away with them'—even if the consequent demand
on rail transport impeded its most effective use for the needs of
a nation at war. Steiner suggests that the animating force
behind this unspeakable collective act was an unacknowledged
repudiation of the demand of humankind that Jewish existence
embodies: the question mark set against its cherished securities
by Moses (he quotes Schoenberg's *Moses und Aaron*), by Karl

[2] Charles Gore, *Jesus of Nazareth* (London, 1929).
[3] 'The Long Life of Metaphor', *Encounter* (Feb. 1987), 55 ff.

Marx—and by Jesus; and quite deliberately he mentions the thorn-crowned Jesus, as if to suggest that in the mocking to which he was submitted, there was a rubbishing of the sort his people were to know many centuries later.

'Oh yet consider it again.' If we obey the imperative here, thrust on us again by this extraordinarily impressive article, we leave our securities behind. Reverence for existing structures, issuing in a readiness to postpone all other considerations to their perpetuation, is called in question. But the consequence is very far from a self-indulgent activism. Rather it is to ask what it was for Jesus to mediate the presence of God in the world, what the manner of that mediation and what the cost. It is in the narratives of Christ's temptation in the wilderness that the manner is initially defined, and the cost outlined. The manner remains a commitment to indirection, the cost a readiness to leave the final verdict to the Father by whom he believed himself sent. As I read Professor Steiner's article, I was reminded of a dominant theme in the understanding of authentic religious experience offered by my revered predecessor in the Norris-Hulse professorship at Cambridge, the late Professor Herbert Farmer. For him awareness of God was compacted of a sense of ultimate demand, and a promise of ultimate succour. For Professor Steiner (if I understand him), Jesus's Jewish inheritance is shown in the way in which he relentlessly presses God's demand upon his hearers: 'But I say unto you—'. Yet at the same time, under the same authority, he offers succour: 'Come unto me, all you that labour, and find refreshment.' But Jesus is only bearer of demand and promise alike because he has archetypally and creatively bowed before the authority of the one, and found his own rest in the promise of the other. So the restlessness that makes him intractable by those who would diminish the ultimacy of his secret by finding in him supposed authorization of their preferences, institutional, cultic, theological.

It was during the Spanish civil war of 1936–9 that a Roman Catholic woman, shocked by the uncritical endorsement of Franco's cause and methods by the majority of her co-religionists, publicly avowed herself horrified by the notion of 'a war to make the world safe for Christianity'. It was a comment of profound wisdom, searching the very foundations of the arguments of all those who would put their confidence in the structures (ultimately coercive) which would, in their judgement, not only safeguard, sustain, and promote, but also mediate Christian belief. Yet Christian belief (something very much more than the vacuous commitment with which it is sometimes identified) is not something to be preserved, let alone mediated, by such means. Rather it is the resonance in the believer of Christ's own faith, charity, and hope, made possible by his own fidelity, to which it is a response, sustained by the promise to which he himself looked, 'And on the third day'. It is in the end as little consonant with intellectual shallowness as it is with the sort of disdainful aloofness that dismisses, for instance, all protest against the acceptance as legitimate of the threat to unleash the whole apparatus of nuclear destruction, as if such protest were no more than the easy indulgence of men and women, kept necessarily apart from the agonizing process of actual decision as it is experienced by those bearing responsibility for the security of the nation.

The State after all is, by its very nature, committed to the use of coercive force to protect those who acknowledge its authority. Moreover the force that it uses is, by its subordination to law, sharply differentiated from violence. It is a commonplace to insist that punishment properly regarded is not an extension of vengeance, but its effective negation. Again, in the tradition of social thought in which Trevor Huddleston stands, that which the founder of the Community of the Resurrection derived from his master in philosophy, T. H. Green,[4] the State is charged with a positive role in advancing the good life. Not for nothing has Green been listed (e.g. by Professor Adam Ulam) among the founding fathers of British socialism. It might seem that, in treating protest as in certain circumstances hardly less than an obligation, there is implicit a rejection of the State's role as positively an engine of the common good. (Green would of course have rejected the use of the mechanical metaphor!)

---

[4] Green's principal work in political theory was his posthumously published *Principles of Political Obligation*. The most interesting recent study of Green is that of the poet Geoffrey Hill, to be found in his volume of critical essays *The Lords of Limit* (London, 1985).

Yet here we have to reckon with two very important limitations. If the State is converted into the effective agent of a party committed to the imposition both in theory and in practice of a system of ideas as perverted as the Nazi doctrines, then the character of the State as *Recht-staat* is gone, and by allowing its hardly limitable coercive powers to be enlisted in service of the humanly destructive, its claim on its citizens' allegiance is forfeit. Further, where in promotion of ends that may be judged valid, and indeed desirable, it commits itself to methods that are at one and the same time hardly controllable in their effect, but involving in their use the near-certainty of the obliteration of hundreds of thousands, if not millions, of human beings, it may well be thought that organized protest has an indispensable role as legitimate, even imperative, human response. The source of positive law has involved itself in lawlessness.

To dismiss such protest out of hand as irresponsible is to ignore the fact that in this case its objective is to be found in what is a matter of human invention. It is not targeted against built-in conditions of human existence: its aim is something that humans beings have brought about, even if it seems almost impossible to be sure that *le premier pas qui coûte* can be precisely dated. We are the prisoners of a terrible inheritance, and if (to borrow an element of Plato's complex imagery) we are bound in a cave, condemned to view only the reflections of the puppets we have fashioned, the fetters that bind us, and indeed the cave which we have hewn out of the rock, are of our own (or our ancestors') making. Finally we are alienated from ourselves, seeing only our shadows, and the moment we are set free by the words of a Socrates or of a Jesus, we are dazzled and confused, preferring the security of our previous bondage and illusion to the terrifying reality of freedom. If the devil of illusion is momentarily cast out, the seven worse than he wait to accompany him back, looking to find the place swept and garnished for their welcome. Memory of the words of Jesus follows naturally on this recollection of the Platonic image. Before we were freed, we did not recognize our bondage for what it was. But now we know, and if we seek to return in fear of freedom, we do so disillusioned and despairing, preferring a security in which we no longer believe to the unknown and unfamiliar. 'Let the dead bury their dead.' 'Take up your cross and come after me.'

The clear implication of this argument is the need to substitute in practice as well as theory an interrogative attitude to the State's claim to know best what is the course of true prudence in matters of defensive armament for one of quiet acceptance. The mood encouraged is one of persistent revolt rather than one of supposedly disciplined acquiescence. If one asked concerning the ensuing relationship envisaged between Church and State, it might be accounted one of tension rather than symbiosis. Certainly this was the direction in which the report of the Church of England Commission, chaired by the Bishop of Salisbury, *The Church and the Bomb* (1983) was pointing, and it is impressive that, notwithstanding the outcome of the debate on the report in the General Synod, responsible representatives of a Church still fettered in many ways by a form of Establishment certainly effete and almost certainly always undesirable should have envisaged such a possibility. It is significant that the Chairman of the Commission was a diocesan bishop, respected as the practitioner of a style of theology much more traditional than that associated, for instance, with the name of Dr John Habgood, the Archbishop of York, perhaps the ablest contemporary defender of the status quo in matters of Anglican Church–State relations in England, and arguably now more at home in the corridors of power than in the world of fundamental theological reflection and questioning.

In his recent book, *Church and Nation in a Secular Age*,[5] Dr Habgood substitutes an extremely able description of existing Church–nation relations in England, sustained by an underlying aversion to any sort of seemingly ill-disciplined or unconsidered activism, for serious engagement with the theology of the Church. The obsessive concentration on the *English* situation (as he sees it), accompanied by an almost total neglect of the contemporaneous Scottish experience, is disappointing in the writing of a man who worked for a period in the Scottish Episcopal Church (as Rector of St John's Church, Jedburgh). It is perhaps not unfair to suggest that to attend to the

[5] John Habgood, Archbishop of York, *Church and Nation in a Secular Age* (London, 1983).

situation north of the Border would have complicated the archbishop's picture, and compelled him to reckon with the fact that radicalism of a sort that he seems to deprecate as 'irresponsible' (and 'irresponsibility' of this kind is a very grievous sin in the primatial judgement) is increasingly marked in the response of the Church of Scotland to the concept of a nuclear deterrent capability. That Church is certainly every bit as much deserving to be characterized as national as is the Church of England. It must also be noted that its radicalism on this issue is shared to an impressive extent by spokesmen of the Roman Catholic and Episcopal churches. It is, of course, fair to point out that geographical proximity to the reality of Trident[6] quickens the imagination in a way in which nearness to Whitehall may deaden it. But it is also arguable that the Scottish situation helps to kindle the resolve to seek a new vision of the Church's being, purged of the irrelevant accretions of centuries of often supine conformity.

On 24 June 1986 there was published in Belfast an impressive Declaration of Faith and Commitment by Christians in Northern Ireland—both Protestant and Roman Catholic.[7] Its inspiration was found in the famous Barmen Declaration of 1934 by a perceptive minority of Protestant Christians in Germany, at a time when the Nazi grip was tightening on that

[6] In the Scottish Christian symposium (the work of a study group convened by the Society, Religion and Technology Project of the Church of Scotland) *Ethics and Defence*, ed. Howard Davis (Oxford, 1986), it is stressed in the preface that 'Scotland is the most heavily armed region of NATO and nuclear issues, both civil and military have been hotly debated.' On most issues of national importance the network of contact between the churches in Scotland are close and relatively effective. The degree of consensus among Church statements on defence and disarmament, for example, is certainly greater than in other parts of the U.K. It amounts to a common mind on a number of crucial issues, including moral condemnation of the threat to use as well as the use of nuclear weapons, opposition to the Trident programme and support for an immediate freeze (ibid. pp. ix and x).

[7] It is well known that the Barmen Declaration was largely written by the great theologian Karl Barth, and is suffused by his radical Christo-monism 'No other name'. The Belfast document is the work both of Protestants and Catholics, responding together to a different situation, but united by their sense of the need to affirm in that situation the lordship of God in Christ, and by Barmen's example.

The Belfast Declaration may be obtained most easily from Inter-church Centre, 48 Elmwood Avenue, Belfast BT9 6AZ.

country. This remarkable Declaration (not much noticed in England or Scotland) by Northern Irish Christians shared with Barmen a determination to stand under the sovereignty of God in Christ. Hence its authenticity as a powerful protest against the falsehoods of competing 'folk religions'. Hence also its significance in a very different context if received as a call to Christian theological renewal to be accomplished not in narrowly sectarian or even confessional terms, but in the light of a Christological vision simultaneously practical and theoretical. There can be no definition of the being and role of the Church that is not achieved by the road of protest in the name of mercy, and I do not mean protest which is tainted by facile, revolutionary indulgence, and which does not draw inspiration from the riddle of Jesus of Nazareth, as writers such as George Steiner have helped us perceive it anew. It is a paradox perhaps to say that it is from such Jewish writers that we receive the sharpest imperative not to discard by means of intellectually facile unitarianism, but rather to review by strenuous intellectual effort, our sense of the mystery of divine condescension in Jesus of Nazareth.

Where Trevor Huddleston and Bruce Kent, who has followed a different path, agree in witness is in their insistence that faith shall not be diminished but enlarged through refusal to confine the Church's reach to a narrowly conceived and deliberately restricted pastoral role. It is ecumenically impressive that through their witness (and I refer here in particular to Bruce Kent) barriers have been broken down. The Catholic has come to appreciate and to learn from the life-style of members of the Society of Friends, and Greenham Common has proved in its way more significant in the ecumenism of the 1980s than the conference room. On Monday 2 March 1987, the widely travelled and experienced Moderator of the General Assembly of the Church of Scotland (Dr Robert Craig), who insisted that he was not a pacifist, visited the 'peace camp' on the Clyde and appeared on BBC 1 (Scotland) praying in a caravan with two campers, both Roman Catholics. It is easy to smile at such apparently trivial manifestations of good will. Yet when they are set in the context of a radical determination to find new forms of churchly existence, less inadequately expressive of the mystery entrusted to the Church's care, they become as highly significant as some of the deliberations, for instance, of ARCIC!

An aged academic is the last person likely to depreciate intellectual concern, the first quickly to disdain disregard of theological values. But 'where is the place of understanding?' It is not to be found in the citadels of embattled orthodoxy, nor among those who crave the dignified security of familiar church structures, or the language of an ancient liturgy. Yet it is not to be found either among those who substitute a febrile activism for sense of human tragedy, who behave spiritually as if Auschwitz had never happened. So we return to the starting-point of these awkwardly constructed reflections: Christ's own continuing interrogation. Theology is the servant of that questioning, or it is nothing.

The place where the questioning must be heard, the Caesarea Philippi of this age, makes the answer no easier for us than for Peter and his fellow men and women. As Professor Steiner most wisely implies, Jesus is too much for us, as he was too much for his disciples. We love to blunt the cutting edge of his teaching, finding, for instance, in his words 'Render unto Caesar the things that are Caesar's, and to God the things that are God's' justification for acting as if God had abdicated all responsibility for the world that Caesar could claim as his, maintaining his divine sovereignty only over a spiritual or churchly realm. But do we suppose for a moment that Jesus believed in any such abdication? Caesar stood under God's dominion, and what he could exact was no more than what that divine dominion permitted. The question how in practice any exaction could be judged legitimate was left open, matter for the human conscience. The riddling tone is resumed in a more sombre setting in the dialogue of Christ and Pilate in John's Passion-narrative: 'Thou hast no power against me at all except it was given thee from above. Therefore he that betrayed me has the greater sin.' But is Pilate (in John's judgement) altogether guiltless? Surely not, even if his sin is less than Judas's. The professional ecclesiastic is always on edge in the presence of the ironic.

It is for the same reason that we have to be on guard in presence of the eager enthusiasm of the modern activist, too quick to forget the tragic reality of human existence. This essay is written in firm conviction of the need for protest regarded not simply as something legitimate but as a moral imperative in face of an acquiescent determinism which refuses to acknowledge the need for re-formation, for revolt. But, as Trevor Huddleston well knows, the way of revolt is not in itself the way of redemption. The latter is something to be received, and received often unwillingly. Peter objected to having his feet washed, and then, in almost lovable confusion, swung round to asking for his whole body to be cleansed— stumbling at the hidden significance of Jesus's menial act. It is on the way of revolt that many will in fact be overtaken by the way of redemption. For Peter found faith not in spite of, but through, exposing himself in muddled folly and ultimately in cowardly denial, when (it must never be forgotten) he had regained enough of his courage (according to the tale) to follow to the high priest's palace. But how few ever reach the place where they may be provoked to such a denial!

Of course, from human history we learn how often out of desperate action, boldly and successfully executed, there comes a new tyranny. Revolutions are only too often the graveyards of the hopes that helped to give them birth. But such recognition should not furnish excuse for acquiescence in established patterns either of injustice or of moral cynicism. Rather it should help those who take the way of protest to realize that for them it is in the end the way that will lead them to judgement and redemption, to the place where they are encountered by the unsearchable mystery of Christ and, being so encountered, through their witness enable others to discern at least a little of his meaning. And here it may be that the lessons to be learnt from George Steiner's article will be rejoined by the teaching of those who within continuing Christian tradition have sought (after the manner of Charles Gore, founder of the Community to which Trevor Huddleston belongs) to deepen our purchase-hold on the secrets of this divine kenosis.

Jesus, in the reality of his self-giving, in the mystery of God's self-giving in him, in his movement from Galilee to Jerusalem to Galilee, in his life, death, and resurrection, remains the only valid *raison d'être* of his Church. In so far as that Church in any of its existing forms diminishes its fidelity to that sovereign inspiration, it invites mistrust, repudiation, contempt even if it seeks to justify that infidelity by reference to historical necessity or even pastoral opportunity. At a meeting held in Edinburgh to consider the theological issues raised by the bitter conflict in Northern Ireland,[8] Dr Garret Fitzgerald issued a warning against the corruption of vision and judgement that might overtake clergy, whether Roman Catholic or Protestant, as a result of their pastoral involvement with members of the IRA or Protestant paramilitary groups. The same judgement might be passed on chaplains ministering to the *Wehrmacht* from 1939–45. Concern for the individual encouraged oblivion of the purposes he served. A Church acquiescent in the status quo, justifying its acquiescence by appeal to pastoral duty, forgets that its pastoral ministry must be fashioned after the model of the 'good shepherd'. It is no generalized caring, but a strenuous, if always imperfect and mutilated, fidelity to the way of Jesus. Similarly apostolate is not a matter of quasi-mechanical transmission, but the kind of conformity to Christ's *Sendung* of which Paul wrote in his *apologia pro vita sua* in 2 Corinthians.

But we crave security: we flee from the reality of crucifixion-resurrection, impatient of the indirection of Christ's resurrection, wishing that he had come down from the Cross that so we might have believed by a faith finally corrupted by its object's betrayal of his mission.

It is because Trevor Huddleston's ministry has been a living and sustained essay towards an authentic fidelity that I venture to offer him these disjointed reflections on Christian existence, given what unity they have by an obsessive conviction that it is to Jesus, author and finisher of our faith,[9] that we must look and look again.

[8] Reported in the *Scotsman* for Monday 9 Mar. 1987.

[9] For further theological treatment of some of the themes in this essay, the reader may be referred to an essay published last year, entitled 'The Evangelical Imagination' (treating of Christ's temptation) in *Religious Imagination: Essays Presented to the Very Rev. Professor John McIntyre*, ed. Prof. J. P. Mackey (Edinburgh, 1986).

The Anti-apartheid Struggle

ABDUL SAMAD MINTY

FATHER HUDDLESTON, as he was, and still is, affectionately known in South Africa, has a very special place in the hearts of millions of Africans in Southern Africa and beyond. Even those who never had an opportunity to meet or even see him, hold Trevor Huddleston in great esteem because of his personal participation in the South African liberation struggle.

Father Trevor Huddleston came to South Africa in 1943, four years after he joined the Community of the Resurrection, a monastic community within the Church of England. He was sent to be priest-in-charge of the Community's mission in Sophiatown, an African township near Johannesburg. Here he came to know the real suffering and frustrations of the African people having to live under a vicious system of white supremacy and race rule.

In 1949 Trevor Huddleston was appointed Provincial of the Community in South Africa and Superintendent of St Peter's School. In 1948 the Afrikaaner-dominated National Party won the white election and began systematically to implement its apartheid programme. He could not remain silent in the face of the new and systematic onslaught of the National Party, and protests over the many injustices, including mass removals and the imposition of Bantu Education, brought him into direct conflict with the regime. It was during this time that Father Huddleston became directly involved in the struggle against apartheid and formed close friendships with African leaders, including Oliver Tambo and Nelson Mandela, who were destined to play a historic role in the African National Congress (ANC) of South Africa.

He emerged as a Gandhi-like figure with enormous moral integrity, standing firmly on principle in open and courageous defiance of the state. He was totally identified with the daily struggle of millions of oppressed Africans. It is in recognition of this unique role that, together with Chief Albert Luthuli and Dr Yusuf Dadoo, Trevor Huddleston was among the first to be awarded the ANC's highest honour, *Isitwalandwe*, on 26 June 1955 at the Congress of the People which adopted the historic Freedom Charter. No English person had played such a vital and important role in the internal anti-apartheid struggle and Father Huddleston personified hope for the future: he demonstrated that it was possible for a white person to understand the suffering of the African masses and to unite with them in trying to rid themselves of racial oppression.

I first met Father Huddleston as a schoolboy when, during his last year in South Africa, he came to our non-racial 'protest' school in Johannesburg to hand out end-of-term prizes and address the school assembly.

In 1956, to everyone's surprise, Father Huddleston was recalled to England by his Community. It was difficult to imagine then, as it was in later years, how someone who had become so much part of South Africa and especially of its growing extra-parliamentary resistance movement should all of a sudden have to leave the country. As a young Christian priest Father Huddleston was fighting for justice, standing side by side with Congress leaders, and for no apparent reason he was withdrawn on superior orders.

Why was he made to leave when he was needed so much inside South Africa? Everyone knew that the regime could not have hoped for anything better than to have this 'meddlesome priest' removed from the country, but did Pretoria really exercise so much influence within the church hierarchy in Britain? What would happen now? Who would take over from him? Was there anyone at all who could replace such a person?

These and other questions lingered long and deeply in the

minds of most of us in South Africa, including schoolchildren who had grown up in the Huddleston era. It was difficult to avoid the conclusion that his departure only made sense as a major concession to the wishes of the apartheid regime. This became yet one more reason to question the role of the Church in South Africa.

However, Pretoria's relief was short-lived: in 1956, upon his return to Britain, Trevor Huddleston's book, *Naught for Your Comfort*, was published. It was widely acclaimed as a powerful indictment of apartheid which also gave a stirring account of the struggle for freedom in South Africa. More than any other book it managed to raise the consciousness of thousands of people in Britain and the rest of the world, challenging and inspiring many of them into action against apartheid.

When I left South Africa to pursue further education and reached London towards the end of 1958, I made early contact with Father Huddleston and went to see him at his Community's house in Holland Park. It was very exciting to see him and learn about various activities being carried out by different organizations in Britain. I also went to see Canon John Collins of St Pauls, who through Christian Action had done so much over many years to inform the British public about the evils of the apartheid system. Canon Collins was well known to the ANC in South Africa as a reliable ally who had also raised substantial sums of money from the public for political trials, including the notorious Treason Trial of 156 Congress leaders who were arrested in 1956. Later I also met the Revd Michael Scott, head of the Africa Bureau in London, who was well known for his representations to the United Nations on behalf of the Namibian people.

In Britain I had the opportunity to attend some of the packed public meetings which Huddleston continued to address throughout the country and to see the impact he made on ordinary people. Of course there were many others who were also active, but there was no doubt that he more than anyone else had brought home to thousands of people the truth about apartheid in South Africa.

However, he was not satisfied with simply drawing attention to what was happening in South Africa, but wanted Britain and the world to take effective action against apartheid. He was convinced that the regime in Pretoria was unlikely to listen to reason and would not voluntarily abandon their policy. If a major violent confrontation was to be avoided it was vital for the international community to apply direct pressure on the regime and its white electorate.

As early as 1957 Father Huddleston had taken initiatives in Britain to organize a cultural and sports boycott of South Africa. He believed that such action 'if widely supported, would make white South Africa acutely aware of its divergence from civilised opinion'. There were some in Britain who did not agree with this and felt that it was better for visits to take place—for actors to try to perform to non-racial audiences, or at least to make sure that there was one special 'non-white' performance in order to compensate for an otherwise 'whites-only' tour.

In 1959 Chief Albert Luthuli, President-General of the ANC, made an international appeal for a boycott of South Africa. Father Trevor Huddleston and Julius Nyerere of Tanganyika were the main speakers at the foundation meeting of the Boycott Movement (later renamed the Anti-apartheid Movement) in London on 26 June 1959, South Africa Freedom Day. Thus began what has turned out to be a long and arduous process of trying to persuade and mobilize British and international public opinion, as well as governments, to support sanctions as an essentially peaceful method to help bring an end to apartheid in South Africa.

Since then, for almost thirty years Trevor Huddleston has tirelessly campaigned at every level to advance the South African people's demand for sanctions. The same arguments have had to be repeated over and over and over again to new listeners as well as old ones—and most of all to those who hold power and do not wish to respond at all, particularly the governments of Britain and the other major Western powers, which seem to be so deeply committed on the side of the apartheid system.

In 1960 Father Huddleston was elected Bishop of Masasi in Tanganyika and thus began another period of intense personal involvement in nation-building and the related problems faced by one of the poorest countries in Africa. Later when he visited Britain he took on the task of interpreting and explaining the aspirations and policies of a newly independent Commonwealth nation: why it operated a one-party system, adopted a socialist *ujamaa* programme, leant heavily towards China, and, after December 1965, broke off diplomatic relations with Britain over Rhodesia's unilateral declaration of independence.

The failure of the British government to act decisively and put down the Rhodesian rebellion amounted in fact to a betrayal of the majority African population of Rhodesia. This created a deep crisis of conscience for many British citizens, including Bishop Huddleston, who spoke out courageously and with considerable anger against Britain's abdication of responsibility for the six million African people who were left under the domination of the illegal Smith regime.

Huddleston returned to England in 1968 as Bishop of Stepney in the East End of London and faced a different range of problems, including growing racist attitudes towards 'immigrants'. In the Stepney area there was a substantial settlement mainly of Asian families from Bangladesh, and once again Bishop Huddleston had to deal with problems of race relations at a different level. Inevitably this also meant that he became directly involved in the work of national organizations concerned with these problems.

But all this did not mean that he had given up working on Southern Africa. Once he returned to Britain Bishop Huddleston resumed his links with the Anti-apartheid Movement (AAM) and played a leading role, especially during the mid-1970s.

In 1975, Bishop Ambrose Reeves (the former Bishop of Johannesburg expelled by the regime for exposing the Sharpeville massacre in 1960) who was President of the AAM, suffered a serious stroke. Trevor Huddleston willingly accepted the responsibilities which resulted from this on behalf of the AAM.

It was the period of the Soweto unrest and the AAM organized a series of activities following the Soweto massacre of 16 June 1976 in which Trevor Huddleston played a leading role.

At this time too, the geo-political situation in Southern Africa was being dramatically transformed as a result of

Angola and Mozambique becoming independent. The Pretoria regime had then invaded Angola and embarked on a programme of military expansion to intimidate and threaten African states in the region. It was trying to acquire a wide range of military equipment from abroad and in July 1976 Bishop Huddleston led a delegation to meet Ministers from the British Foreign Office and the Defence Ministry to press for the strict implementation of the arms embargo against South Africa. Four days later, on 12 July 1976, Trevor Huddleston gave the keynote address at a rally in Westminster Central Hall on the theme: 'Freedom for South Africa: Where does Britain Stand?'

During 1977 he continued to be in the forefront of the AAM's major campaigns and, following the killing of Steve Biko in September 1977 and banning of the South African Students' Organization (SASO) and other black conscious-ness organizations, he addressed a mass protest rally on 25 October 1977, again in the Westminster Central Hall.

In January 1978 Bishop Huddleston addressed a special meeting in the House of Commons called to prepare for the United Nations International Anti-apartheid Year which was to start on 21 March 1978. A co-ordinating committee was established and several organizations worked together under the leadership of the AAM and the United Nations Association to promote nation-wide activities.

Later in 1978 Trevor Huddleston was appointed archbishop and moved to the Indian Ocean island of Mauritius. However, in April 1981 he was elected President of the AAM following the death of Bishop Ambrose Reeves. Despite being based in Mauritius, Trevor Huddleston played a key role in a number of major initiatives.

Following the independence of Zimbabwe in 1980 and the coming to power of Prime Minister Mugabe, the South African regime became even more isolated and began to embark on a further programme of militarization. All the independent states in the region were threatened with war unless they abandoned their anti-apartheid policy.

The AAM therefore organized a three-day international conference in London in March 1982 on 'Southern Africa: The Time to Choose'. At the invitation of the archbishop the

Nigerian government sent a high-level delegation led by its Vice-President, and other participants included representatives from several overseas countries including some from North America and Western Europe as well as the United Nations. This conference was a major breakthrough in several respects, with the Opening Session being addressed by the leaders of the British Labour and Liberal Parties as well as by the Secretary-General of the Commonwealth, Shridath Ramphal. The conference paid particular attention to the increasingly aggressive role of South Africa throughout the region and called for effective international action in support of the liberation movements in South Africa and Namibia and for the front-line and other independent African states.

On the Sunday after the conference over 15,000 people took part in a demonstration in Trafalgar Square, and on the same day the London office of the ANC was the target of a bomb attack. This was the first such action in Britain. The conference clearly represented a serious threat to the apartheid regime and its supporters. On the following day Bishop Huddleston met Lord Carrington at the Foreign Office. He raised the question of the bomb attack calling for an immediate investigation—and was assured that the government would take urgent action; but to this day no one has been apprehended. He also conveyed the conclusions of the conference to the Foreign and Commonwealth Secretary, who undertook to study them but repeated that the British government did not believe in sanctions against South Africa. The fact that this meeting took place also reflected the growing influence of the movement under the leadership of Bishop Huddleston.

On 5 November 1982 the bishop was honoured by the United Nations, when he was awarded its Gold Medal for his contribution to the international campaign against apartheid and particularly the demand for sanctions against South Africa. When he addressed the General Assembly on that occasion the hall was unusually silent, with the delegates listening to every word. Like so many other speeches made by the bishop, this one conveyed his deep personal concern and involvement in the struggle against apartheid as well as his impatience at the lack of effective international action.

In August 1982 Trevor Huddleston launched the International Declaration for the release of Nelson Mandela and all other political prisoners and was invited to many events and activities organized to honour the great South African ANC leader. In October 1984 he presented to the UN Secretary-General in New York the first batch of the Free Mandela Petitions, signed by over half a million persons around the world.

In April 1983 Trevor Huddleston retired as archbishop and returned from Mauritius to England, and since then has devoted himself to work on Southern Africa. He has always been concerned that whatever was done in Britain and abroad about Southern Africa should be undertaken after close consultation with the leaders of the liberation movements and the front-line states. In January 1984 he visited Zambia, Zimbabwe, Botswana, Mozambique, and Tanzania and met with the leaders of these countries as well as with the liberation movements, including his close friend President Oliver Tambo of the ANC.

Even for someone familiar with the record and standing of Trevor Huddleston in Africa and with the affection that exists for him throughout the region it was a pleasant surprise to see the deep and genuine warmth and generous welcome that was extended to him. In two of the countries the presidents were away from their capitals and special aircraft were made available to transport him for their respective meetings. The conversations were relaxed and often quite long. The African leaders gave the bishop detailed information about current developments—and asked for his assessment of the situation in Southern Africa as well as the prospects for positive international action.

In Botswana South African exiles and others who had travelled across the border specially to meet him organized a spontaneous party in his honour. In Harare, after the church service in which he participated, crowds gathered to see him. Cabinet Ministers telephoned his hotel and arranged to meet him, recalling how much he had inspired them during their youth. At Maputo airport the Governor who welcomed him found that he did not need his interpreter, and they spoke easily in Swahili, which they had both learnt earlier in Tanzania.

Trevor Huddleston was able to return to Britain and carry on with his work in the knowledge that what he was doing had the full support of those most directly affected by the situation in Southern Africa.

On 24 May 1984 the Zambian government announced that Bishop Trevor Huddleston had been granted Zambia's highest award, the Order of Freedom, First Class.

Meanwhile P. W. Botha had decided to visit Britain and several other European capitals during May–June 1984, in an effort to end South Africa's international isolation. The AAM protested at the British invitation, and Trevor Huddleston wrote to Mrs Margaret Thatcher, outlining the reasons why the visit should not take place. On the eve of the Botha visit the Prime Minister met Bishop Huddleston at Downing Street and he was able to convey personally why it was a mistake to invite Botha to Britain. Trevor Huddleston later addressed the major 'No to Botha' demonstration that took place in London in June 1984.

Bishop Huddleston is best known for his work on South Africa, but he has always searched for ways to focus attention on the much-neglected question of Namibia. In May 1985 he had a special meeting with Sir Geoffrey Howe, the British Foreign and Commonwealth Secretary, regarding Namibia, and he has made numerous representations to the British and other governments on the subject. The President of SWAPO, Sam Nujoma, is a close friend and they consult regularly about developments.

In recent years there has hardly been any major activity of the Anti-apartheid Movement without the direct involvement of its President, Trevor Huddleston. The activities range from letter-writing to protest meetings as well as extensive travel: too many to list. They include convening an international Multi-faith Consultation on Apartheid in London; joining a procession of fifty mayors to Downing Street on 11 June 1985, calling for the release of Nelson Mandela; addressing 100,000 people in Trafalgar Square with Jesse Jackson and Oliver Tambo in November 1985; addressing 250,000 people on Clapham Common in June 1986 at an Anti-apartheid music festival; giving evidence to the Commonwealth Eminent

Persons Group on Southern Africa; lobbying the British government, Members of Parliament, and Commonwealth governments both before and after the 1985 Commonwealth Summit in the Bahamas and the subsequent London Review Meeting of August 1986.

Since January 1984, in addition to the front-line states he has visited Australia, New Zealand, Canada, the USA, the USSR, Bermuda, Austria, Belgium, Norway, and Sweden. In most of these countries he has met with the most senior government leaders, including Heads of government. He has been to India twice, and on both occasions had extensive discussions with Prime Minister Rajiv Gandhi.

It is impossible to know how much these and other leaders and their governments have been influenced by Trevor Huddleston, but there is no doubt about their readiness to meet with him and seek his views. But his influence goes beyond governments, as is demonstrated, for example, by the level of anti-apartheid public opinion in Britain. It is perhaps too early to judge exactly how much the Anti-apartheid Movement owes to Trevor Huddleston, who has been involved in its work since its inception in 1959, but there is no doubt that it would not have achieved as much without his inspiring leadership.

A somewhat less well-known aspect of Trevor Huddleston's work is his long association with the late John Collins and the International Defence and Aid Fund for Southern Africa. When Trevor Huddleston was in South Africa and needed funds for political trials it was Canon Collins who raised much of the money. During the four-year long Treason Trial Bishop Ambrose Reeves, based in Johannesburg, co-operated with Canon Collins until 1960. Thereafter both Ambrose Reeves and Trevor Huddleston maintained close personal contact with Canon Collins and kept in touch with the work of the Fund. When the Fund changed its structure Trevor Huddleston was appointed among the first group of trustees and was elected chairman in February 1983 after the death of Canon Collins. The Fund was banned by the South African regime in 1964, but it has managed to survive and grow over the years, taking on new and more difficult responsibilities as and when they have arisen in Southern Africa.

Trevor Huddleston joined the battle against the system of racial supremacy in South Africa in the streets of Sophiatown and Orlando in 1943 and emerged as an outspoken and prophetic opponent of apartheid. For over four decades he has been actively involved on the side of the South African liberation struggle, courageously proclaiming the truth. His early and repeated appeals for effective non-violent action to help end apartheid have been rejected time and again by the major Western powers, which have continued to collaborate with the Pretoria regime.

Remembering Trevor Huddleston's seventy-fifth birthday affords one the opportunity to reflect on the enormous personal contribution that he has made to the anti-apartheid struggle, both within South Africa and abroad. At the same time one cannot help but think about the massive suffering endured by millions of African people in Southern Africa that could so easily have been avoided had Britain and the West heeded his early warnings. Even now, with increasing violence being unleashed by the apartheid regime throughout the region, threatening an impending catastrophe, the Western powers persist with their appeasement policies.

In one sense Trevor Huddleston's prophetic role made him ahead of his time. In a different world, together with outstanding leaders like Mahatma Gandhi and Mwalimu Nyerere, he would long ago have been awarded the Nobel Peace Prize. His challenge to the world always was, and remains, essentially a moral one: fearlessly to assert the dignity and worth of human beings and to live and work, through action, for the early destruction of the evil system of apartheid.

We are thankful for having Trevor Huddleston.

Trevor Huddleston

ROBIN DENNISTON

OFTEN when moral theory is being discussed a distinction is drawn between what a person does and what he or she is. Sometimes it seems appropriate to define a person by what they do, perhaps because there may be little else, or little evidence of anything else, other than their observed or inferred activities, on which to base a reputation. But for others, a definition in terms of activity seems an inadequate description, and the definition of such people (what they stand for, how people react to them, their place in history) is seen to be more than the sum of their actions. The distinction itself is rather woolly because, while a person is obviously different from the sum of his or her activities, each observer will take a different view of these differences.

The distinction between identity and activity is more apparent when a person's actions do not seem to bear out their personality. If there is a regular and extreme mismatch between identity and action one may be looking at a case of schizophrenia, but if the match is total, so that one is another way of looking at the same phenomenon as the other, you have a person of rare sanity and consistency. And where the actions over a long and active life are consistent with each other in the context of a changing life and the development of events, there you are likely to find a personality and achievement of significance.

Which is cause and which effect? Does identity define character or does activity determine identity? While actions clearly affect character and identity they do not determine it, because it is possible to have high virtues without any notable context to display them. Such a person's influence cannot be measured merely by the effect of their actions. In their character resides a propensity to heroic action which the circumstances of a particular life make it impossible to carry out. The self is greater than its means of expression. An active and engaged public figure who has also taken the vows of poverty and obedience points up this distinction—which can therefore be seen to be of relevance in the life of Trevor Huddleston. But the difference between his two lives is far from being paradoxical, and in his case (and that of other rare spirits) the spiritual life fuels the busy days of a lifelong campaign for human dignity. Far from being a mismatch, there is an identity between what he does, what he has a propensity for doing, and what he is. Anyone who has known him or worked with him knows this.

Many others know him as a preacher, others still as the author of a book (*Naught for Your Comfort*) still regarded as giving as true a picture of the apartheid situation in South Africa as anything which has appeared since. If that is so it may partly be because of its almost agonizing intensity.

This book, written from the heart of the Africa I love, would be incomplete if I did not somehow see it in the context of this sudden, unwanted, but inevitable departure: 'Partir, c'est mourir un peu' . . . and I am in the process of dying: in the process 'every hour'. The thing about such a death, the quality of it, is to heighten the loveliness of what one is leaving behind . . . I must try to discover and relate that strange but deeply real truth which so many have experienced: the witchery of Africa—the way it lays its hold on your heart and will not let you go.

It was the vow of obedience, as well as the South African government's pressure, which drove Huddleston into exile. The vow of obedience was given in 1940 in Mirfield, and in 1955 it was this alone, he writes, 'that gives a man the strength, when he most needs it, to die by parting from what he loves. Nothing else could have torn me away from Africa at that moment.' The parting must have been almost unbearable. 'What does it mean,' he goes on, 'this real agony of parting? Why does it cost so much?' At the end of this section he writes of 'the darkness of the years that lie ahead'. The twelve years of life in South Africa had ended in the death of departure and exile. He is, I believe, still in exile and still mourning, despite the excitements and achievements of later years.

Exile, death, departure: disappointment too. Despite the evidence and the appeal of his book—which went on to sell all over the world—public opinion was only slightly stirred. The social, economic, and spiritual crimes he and others revealed are all happening a long way from the centres of world politics. Now that scenes of township unrest and police action are banned from the media, we all in some degree withdraw our concern. Huddleston himself has become one of the leading figures in the world-wide anti-apartheid movement, but, despite all his gifts as an advocate and his consistent position, passionately expressed, on all racial issues, change is slow in coming. The present situation could well daunt a man of lesser inner strength, or anyone whose identity, propensities, and activities are less well integrated than his.

INDEX